MW00910693

Preface

The following 11 lesson curriculum is designed to give content information for the instructor of this course. The lesson plan is suitable to use for youth through adult. The material should be studied and thoroughly understood by the instructor before being presented and should be age appropriate.

Kingdom Academy Curriculum

Introduction

The purpose of Old Town Kingdom Academy is very specific. Our church has an effective and vibrant infant, children and youth program teaching the Christian faith and practices. However, our children and youth interface with the world every day. The majority of the people they have contact with, whether in person, internet, media, or through literature, are not Christians.

Jesus told us that the entrance to heaven is a narrow path and very few are on it. (Matthew 7:13-14) Most of our children and youth interface with a fallen world on a daily basis. It is during the school years that our youth develop their beliefs about how life works. The problem is nonbelievers are molding our children and youth into the world's belief system.

While we want our children to respect and honor their teachers, many of the teachers are not Christians or simply must teach a curriculum that is very different than what our families and church believe. These teachers, either by mandate or choice, often teach our children the opposite of what we, as Christians believe. Yet their impressionable minds believe what their teacher tells them.

This academy is designed to teach and give facts, evidence and truth for a biblical view in the areas where the teachers often give opposing views of the parents or church. We want to give students factual evidence so they will have the tools necessary to withstand the attack against their faith.

THE BIBLE

All of Christianity is built upon the authenticity of the Bible as being the Word of God.

Even though it is the Word of God, men wrote it. They wrote the Bible under God's supervision. They were inspired of God as they wrote it (2 Timothy 3:16).

Inspiration means the process of being mentally stimulated to do or write something for God as the Bible writers were.

The Scriptures are authored by God in such a way that the personality and abilities of the biblical writers was without error and was correct in every detail. Therefore, the Scriptures are the product of both God and man.

The Bible is broken down into two halves, the Old Testament and the New Testament.

There are 66 books that comprise the Bible. There are 39 O.T. books and 27 N.T. books.

The O.T. is before the birth of Jesus, the N.T. is after His birth.

The Bible is the only place we find a clear and reasonable purpose and meaning of life.

   a. How we got here
   b. What is the purpose of life
   c. Is there life after death
   d. Why is the world full of evil

The Bible has been faithfully passed down for over 3,400 years.

Actually 40 authors wrote 66 books during a period of over 1,500 years.

Why believe the Bible?   It claims to be the Word of God (Jeremiah 1:9; 2 Peter 1:21; I Corinthians 2:13).

Why doesn't everyone believe the Bible? (2 Corinthians 4:3-4)

The Bible and its teachings were attacked from the very first writers and still is today. The more it is attacked the more people read and believe it.

Why study the Bible?

   1. Bible study is necessary and essential for Christian growth (I Peter 2:2).
   2. Bible study is essential to become spiritually mature (Hebrews 5:11-14).
   3. Bible study is essential for spiritual effectiveness (2 Timothy 3:16-17).
   4. The Bible will structure your thinking.
   5. The Bible points out sin so we can walk away from it.

***The Bible is superior to the teachings of any other book in history. The Bible contains all truth.

We live in a time where many people do not think there is any objective truth; it is all situational. The Bible contains all truth.

The Bible is indestructible. It has always been hated by some and cherished by others.

The Bible has been faithfully passed down through the centuries. The Dead Sea Scrolls is proof of that. These scrolls were buried for two thousand years and were found in 1947. Compare the Old Testament findings with our Old Testament today and you will see no changes.

The Bible is scientifically correct. There are different categories of science:

a. Observable science
b. Historical science

Observable science is a theory which can be proven because it can be:

1. Observed
2. Measured
3. Repeated

Historical science, because of its nature, must reach into the past and make assumptions or theories. This is necessary because none of the scientists or any of us were there in the distant past.

The Bible never conflicts with pure observable science. Historical scientists often make some incredible statements. They base their belief on false or incorrect evidence to substantiate their theory, and then call it science.

Evidence to prove the Bible is truly God's Word.

1. The Bible was written by 40 different human writers over 50 generations. Many of these writers had no opportunity to collaborate with each other and yet, there are no contradictions in their writings. They agreed on many themes like morality (which certainly has changed drastically in a few generations in our society), child rearing, husband and wife relations, the character of God, the way of salvation and the birth, life, death and resurrection of the Savior of mankind, in minute details.
2. The Bible was scientifically correct hundreds of years in advance of man's knowledge.
   a. God gave Israel hygiene laws in Deuteronomy 23:12-13: dig a pit for waste. In many countries they didn't dig latrines and as a result typhoid, cholera and dysentery killed millions.
   b. God told the Jewish fathers to circumcise their sons on the eighth day (Gen. 17:12). The important blood clotting vitamin K2 in blood is not manufactured in a baby's intestinal tract in normal amounts until the 5th to 7th days after their birth. A second element necessary for blood clotting is prothrombin. The presence of this element decreases in an infant for the first 3 days of its life, then suddenly spurts to a maximum level on the eighth day, after which it settles to its norm for the rest of the child's life.
   c. The book of Isaiah (40:22) speaks of the circle of the earth long before anyone knew it was circular and not flat.
   d. The book of Ecclesiastes (1:7) stated all the rivers run into the sea; yet the sea is not full, nor does it run back again, no one knew this at that time.
   e. Job 26:7. He stretches out the north over the empty place, and hangs the earth upon nothing. No cultures understood who or how the earth was held in place or hung in space.
3. Prophecy:
   Can anyone select a large metropolitan area and predict in advance, and in detail, how that city will be destroyed? The Bible did, and not with just one city, but many.

Ezekiel, as a captive in Babylon, made some very specific predictions about the seacoast metropolis of Tyre. Ezekiel 26:3-14 predicts the destruction of Tyre in detail (592-570 BC).

Nebuchadnezzar came against Tyre in 585 BC (fulfilling vs 26:7). The siege lasted until 573 BC. When he broke down the gates of the city he found most of the population had escaped by ship to a city they had built on an island about a half mile out into the sea.

In 333 BC, Alexander III in a southern campaign, demolished old Tyre and used the materials and dirt to build a causeway to the new city which had been built out in the water. The island city was destroyed and the materials cast into the sea (fulfilling 26:12). This fulfilled Ezekiel's prophecy exactly as predicted.

Biblical prophesies of destroyed cities or populations are: The city of Samaria (Hosea 13, Micah 1) cities of Gaza and Ashkelon (Amos 1; Jeremiah 47; Zephaniah 2), kingdom of Edom and its capitol, Petra (Isaiah 34; Jeremiah 49; Ezekiel 25 and 35) the city of Damascus (Isaiah 17:1).

***The prophecies of the birth, life, death and resurrection of Jesus Christ.
- His birth location (Micah 5:2)
- Method of birth (Isaiah 7:14).
- Time of birth (Daniel 9:25-26)
- His lineage (Isaiah 11:1- Jeremiah 23:5) and many more prophecies; actually 333 in all, including His death, burial and resurrection.

4. The Bible simply works. The instructions on raising children, on marriage, on forgiving others simply work. For the person who has come to Christ and experienced the personal relationship between God and themselves, no additional proofs of the Bible are needed.

5. Archaeological evidences that have been discovered, corroborated the kings, cities and civilizations the Bible talks about. No discovery has ever been found to disprove any facts written in Scripture. Archaeology is the study of human history and prehistory through the excavation of sites and the analysis of artifacts and other physical remains.

6. Writings outside the Bible have only corroborated the locations, and events spoken of in the Bible.

7. Studying the lives of the men who wrote the Bible shows they were honest and sincere. The fact that they were willing to die often excruciating deaths for what they believed testifies that these ordinary yet honest men truly believed God had spoken to them. William Tyndale was burned at the stake in 1536 for translating the Bible from Hebrew and Greek into English so the common person could read it. He was charged and convicted of heresy.

8. The evidence that the Bible is truly God's Word is the indestructibility of the Bible. Because of its importance and its claim to be the very Word of God, the Bible has suffered more vicious attacks and attempts to destroy it than any other book in history. From early Roman Emperors like Diocletian, through Communist dictators and on to modern-day atheists and agnostics, the Bible has withstood and outlasted all of its attackers and is still today the most widely published book in the world.

9. The Bible has had civilizing effect on societies.
The Bible's message has elevated many 'barbarians' to decency. It is the basis of English Common Law, the American Bill of Rights and the constitution of great modern democracies such as the United Kingdom and the United States, which has inspired many other democracies. The Bible has inspired the noblest of literature—from Shakespeare, Milton, Pope, Scott, Coleridge and Kipling, to name a few—and the art of such as Leonardo da Vinci, Michelangelo, Raphael and Rembrandt. The Bible has inspired the music of Bach, Handel, Haydn, Mendelssohn and Brahms.

10. The winding down of the earth is biblical. The universal tendency of things to run down and to fall apart shows that the universe had to be 'wound up' at the beginning. The earth is not eternal. This is proven by the Second Law of Thermodynamics.

Kingdom Quiz (The Bible)

1. How many books are in the Bible?
2. Who wrote the Bible?
    a. God
    b. Men
    c. God and men
3. What does inspiration mean?
4. Is the Bible always correct?
5. What is the difference between the Old Testament and the New Testament?
6. Why are there so many people who do not believe the Bible?
7. What are the Dead Sea Scrolls and why are they so important?
8. Is the Bible scientifically correct?
9. What is archaeology and why does it help prove the Bible is true?

The God of Creation

How did our world and all of creation begin?

Genesis 1 tells us God created heaven and earth by simply speaking it into existence. There was no big bang theory. God simply spoke everything into existence in 6 days.

An article was published in *New Scientist,* May 22, 2004, An Open Letter to the Scientific Community which stated "The Big Bang Theory" today relies on a growing number of hypothetical entities, things that we have never observed. Inflation, dark matter and dark energy are the most prominent examples. But the Big Bang Theory can't survive without these fudge factors. What is more, the Big Bang Theory can boast of no quantitative predictions that have subsequently been validated by observation. Initial signatories: 33 scientists from 10 countries. Subsequent signatories: 500 (218 scientists and engineers- 187 independent researchers- 105 others).

This was the beginning of the universe not the beginning of God. God has always existed.

Day 1: God created the heavens (outer space) and earth.

Day 2: God created the sky (the atmosphere between the earth's water and clouds above).

Day 3: God created dry land.

Day 4: God created all the stars and planets.

Day 5: God created life that lives in water and the birds.

Day 6: God created all living creatures, which includes dinosaurs, on dry land. Then He created man to oversee His creation.

Day 7: God rested.

Over the last 150-200 years, some people believe the word or meaning for a day could be interpreted as thousands of years.

How long was a day in Genesis? (DVD Is Genesis History 18:00-23:30)

Think about this: God created a fully functioning universe in six days. Adam was a fully functioning man in his twenties in one day. All physical indications show he was around for twenty years but God created him whole and grown in a day. The chicken wasn't created from an egg but was a fully functioning grown chicken on day six. The sun, moon and the rest of the universe were necessary for Adam to live, and it was created in a day. Genesis 1:5 also speaks of "the evening and morning of the first day. This implies one sunrise and one sunset. A fully functioning universe that appears to have been around for who knows how long was created in a day. Some scientists attempt to age the earth because of its appearance. Their numbers are all over the scale because they are using a false premise that all evolved or believing the Big Bang Theory as the origin of the universe.

Man and all creation were to eat plants only. This was changed after the flood. Now for man every living thing that was alive, as well as the green plants, was for eating (Genesis 9:3-4).

However, there is fossil record showing us that after the fall and before the flood much of the animal kingdom became carnivorous.

On the 6th day of creation God created Adam and Eve in His image (Genesis 1:26-27). Adam looked like us, not like a cave man as some would think.

God created the earth, planets and all living life in 6 days approximately 6,000 years ago, or about 4004 BC. The earth was not created millions or billions of years ago.

Many believe what some scientists tell us about the age of the earth then they try to fit God's Word into that belief.

Many believers struggle with the age of the earth not being millions of years old because that it is all they have ever heard. So the church has come up with a compromise such as 'day-age-theory' or 'gap theory' or the 'progressive creation' view. They are all attempts to fit millions of years into the Bible.

The belief that the earth is millions of years old is the major reason for belief in evolution. Deep time i.e. millions of years is the slippery slope to unbelief. Most people have no idea why they think the earth is billions of years old. It's just assumed because that's all they hear. Deep time is the foundation for all evolutionary thinking that must be demolished first before we tackle evolution.

Breaking News!!! The earth is not old like you have been told and taught.

How do we know the age of the Earth?

There are two views to answer that question:

a. Young-earth believers say the age of the earth and universe is about 6,000 years.

b. Old-earth believers believe the age of the earth to be about 4.5 billion years and a universe about 14 billion years old.

The young earth people get there ages from the Bible. Genesis 1 tells us that the earth was created on the first day of creation. From there, we can begin to calculate the age of the earth. The age of the earth can be estimated by following the genealogies from Adam to Abraham in Genesis 5 through 11, then adding in the time from Abraham to today. If we add up the dates from Adam to Abraham, we get about 2,000 years. Whether Christian or secular, most scholars would agree that Abram lived about 2,000 B.C. (4,000 years ago). Adding all together brings us to 6,000 years.

Where did the old earth view come from? For the first 1700 years of the church the earth was always considered to have been created about 4000 B.C. The millions of years view took hold in geology in the 1800's when men like Abraham Werner, James Hutton, William Smith, George Cuvier, and Charles Lyell used their interpretations of geology as the standard, rather than the Bible. Lyell was a Deist.

He believed in some sort of creating intelligence but didn't believe the biblical account of creation. He wrote the book, "The Principles of Geology." Lyell is considered by many to be the father of modern geology. Charles Darwin used this book as the basis of his 'Theory of Evolution.' Werner estimated the age of the earth at about one million years. From these men and others came the consensus view that the geologic layers were laid down slowly over long periods of time based on the rates at which we see them accumulating today.

Hutton said, "The past history of our globe must be explained by what can be seen to be happening now. No powers are to be employed that are not natural to the globe, no action to be admitted except those of which we know the principle."

This viewpoint is called naturalistic uniformitarianism, and it excludes any major catastrophes such as Noah's flood.

Thinking biblically, we can see that the global flood in Genesis 6-8 would wipe away the concept of millions of years, for this flood would explain massive amounts of fossil layers. A global flood would rip up many of the previous rock layers and redeposit them elsewhere, destroying the previous fragile contents.

What took place around Mount St. Helen, in 1980, clearly reveals this principle (Is Genesis History DVD :24-3:23).

With the development of radiometric dating in the early 20th century, the age of the earth expanded radically. However, there is growing scientific evidence that radiometric dating methods are completely unreliable, and shown to be wildly in error. The age of the earth debate ultimately comes down to this foundational question: are we trusting man's imperfect and changing ideas and assumptions about the past? Or, do we trust God's perfectly accurate eyewitness account of the past.

God created everything out of nothing by speaking it into existence.

He created the heavens and earth as a visible expression of His glory, beauty, and power (Psalm 19:1). The heavens scream of a creator.

God placed in the heart of every man the knowledge of a creator and it is man's responsibility to discover who that is (Romans 1:18-20). Those who do not believe in God have no excuse.

Albert Einstein said, "The harmony of natural law reveals an intelligence of such superiority that compared with it all the systematic thinking of human beings is utterly insignificant."

The Anthropic Principle is the law of human existence. This principle is a clear proof of God. The principle shows our universe was fine-tuned to allow for life, (water, oxygen, temperature, sun and moon etc.). This principle tells us the earth could not have simply randomly evolved.

This law means the extreme improbability that so many variables would align by chance in our favor has led scientists and philosophers to propose instead that it was God who providentially engineered the universe to suit our specific needs. This is the Anthropic Principle: that the universe appears to have been fine-tuned for our existence.

God expects all of His creation to give Him glory.

God created the earth to provide a place where His purpose and goals for human kind could be fulfilled.

He created mankind with the ability to have a free will, to choose to follow and believe in Him or not.

Because Adam sinned, we now inherit that sin. That is why Jesus came to pay for our sins. Adam's sin changed the spiritual make-up of the earth and all born after him inherit his sin nature.

This sin grew so rapidly as the earth was populated that God came to a point that He said, "it is enough" and the entire earth was destroyed by water except one man and his wife and three sons and their wives. The flood totally changed the make-up of the earth that God created (Genesis 6:11-17; 7:11-16).

What about dinosaurs?

The Bible provides proof that man and dinosaurs lived during the same time:

Biblical creationists believe that man and dinosaurs lived at the same time because God, a perfect eyewitness to history, said that He created man and land animals on Day 6 (Genesis 1:24-31). Dinosaurs are land animals, so logically they were created on Day 6.

The fossil record proves man and dinosaurs lived on earth at the same time.

What is a fossil? A fossil is the remains or impression of a prehistoric organism preserved in petrified form or as a mold or cast of rock. The fossil record proves a catastrophic event took place and plants and animals were fossilized immediately, not with slow deposits over a long period of time, or uniformitarianism.

Let me tell you something about the collecting of evidence. The earth is filled with evidence, but evidence doesn't speak. It must be interpreted. Both sides (young earth and old earth) have the same evidence, but their worldview totally affects how they view and analyze that evidence. Each side begins with a deep seated premise. The old earth people begin with the belief of slow changes in the earth's surface over billions of years with no major cataclysmic events taking place.

The young earth people believe the earth was created by God approximately 6,000 years ago in six days.

However, old earth believers have another factor that must be considered. Most believe in the evolution of the species, to maintain that belief they must believe the billions of years theory. There is no God in their humanistic worldview. With that belief they will interpret all evidence with that mindset.

Young earth people must have 6,000 years of age to conform to the teaching of Scripture.

Both have a worldview that affects how they view and analyze the evidence.

The fatal flaw of uniformitarianism, which tells us we can view processes in the present and extrapolate those backwards to tell us the past history. This DVD clip clearly demonstrates the grave error of uniformitarianism, how worldwide flood would wipe clear the entire earth.

Why don't we find many fossils of dinosaurs and man together? In most cases, dead things decompose or get eaten. They just disappear and nothing is left. The 2004 tsunami in Southeast Asia was a shocking reminder of the speed with which water and other forces can eliminate all trace of bodies, even when we know where to look. According to the United Nation's office of the Special Envoy for Tsunami Recovery, nearly 43,000 tsunami victims were never found.

Just because animals are not found together does not mean they do not live in the same world at the same time. Would you want to live close to a dinosaur?

The book of Job refers to a creature called behemoth (Job 40:15).

The fact that dinosaur femur soft tissues have been found and described as "still squishy" and contain recognizable blood cells also confirms the recency of dinosaur fossil deposition.

DNA has been found in dinosaur bone cells, which means they must be relatively young. Estimates of DNA stability put its upper limit of survival at 125,000 years at 0 degree C, 17,500 years at 10 degree C, and 2,500 years at 20 degree C. A recent paper on DNA shows that it might be able to last, under certain circumstances, as much as 400 times longer in bone. But there is no way DNA could last the evolutionary time since dinosaur believed extinction by the old earth people. While this does not prove a young earth, it certainly disproves the 70 million years of its extinction the old earth evolutionists proclaim. DNA evidence found in these bones disproves the old earth theory.

Carbon-14 has been found in dinosaur bone. C-14 is used to date organic matter (not rocks), and it has a short 5,730 year half-life. After about 100,000 years, there should be no detectable C-14 left. Yet, C-14 levels hundreds of times above the equipment detection limit have been found.

Before the word "dinosaur" was invented, creatures fitting the description of dinosaurs were mentioned in the Bible- the Behemoth of Job 40:15-41 and the Leviathan of Job 41; Psalm 74:4 and Isaiah 27:1.

Dinosaurs have been used to promote the belief in evolution for decades yet they actually fit a recent biblical creation viewpoint far better than a million-of-years evolutionary perspective.

The book, The Travels of Marco Polo, is the written record which chronicles the adventures and travels that Marco Polo experienced while exploring the eastern world. In his book, Marco Polo reports what he describes as "huge serpents". In Book 2, chapter 49, pg. 158-160 he clearly describes dinosaurs or leviathans in the years 1271-1298. The Bible talks about them being serpents in Isaiah 27:1.

It's clear to me what happened to them. A particular organ in the dinosaur was used for several medicinal uses and worked well. Just like, in our day the rhinoceros has been tranquilized to saw off their ivory horns to preserve the animal from being poached, the dinosaurs were hunted to extinction.

Only a fool will reject our Creator and Savior (Psalm 53:1), and those who refuse to see it and desperately seek some evolutionary way of explaining it are without excuse (Romans 1:20).

Kingdom Quiz (The God of Creation)

1. God created man and woman and gave them a _____ _____.

2. What happened to all humanity when Adam sinned?

3. How old is the earth?

4. What event took place that totally changed the physical structure of the earth?

5. What event took place that totally changed the spiritual makeup of the earth?

6. What does the anthropic principle tell us about the universe?

7. What day of creation were fish created?

8. What day of creation was Adam created?

9. Did Adam look like a cave man?

The Great Deception - The Theory of Evolution

The evolutionary theory states that natural selection and mutations working over millions of years formed all the diversity of life we see in the world today. Genesis, however, says God created animals fully-formed, "according to their kinds." When one studies the similarities and differences of animals, a better explanation is that each created kind possesses enormous potential for genetic change. These changes within kinds have often been pointed to as arguments for evolution, but changes between kinds have not been observed. Instead of a single tree of life growing from a common ancestor, each created kind has its own unique tree.

There is no empirical proof of this theory. It is all based on circumstantial evidence not direct evidence.

The definition of the word 'empirical' is: based on verifiable evidence or by observation rather than theory or pure logic.

Evolution not only cannot be proven but it defies logic:

- Nothing gave rise to something at an alleged 'big bang'.
- Non –living matter gave rise to life.
- Single-celled organisms gave rise to many-celled complex organisms.
- Invertebrates gave rise to vertebrates.
- Ape-like creatures gave rise to man.
- Non-intelligent and amoral matter gave rise to intelligence and morality.

I will progressively be showing how all evidence for a young earth is marginalized or suppressed by the scientific community because it does not match their narrative or belief system (for example DVD "Is Genesis History" 23:41-29:15).

The entire belief of evolution is based upon circumstantial evidence. Much of this so called evidence has been cherry picked from other opposing, unspoken of evidence.

Circumstantial evidence is evidence that is not conclusive.

A theory is a supposition or an idea to explain something or point toward a belief but is not a fact.

Because not everyone wants to believe in or follow God, the world has come up with another belief system. It is called Evolution and our youth will be taught this in school, in movies, television, books, music, and magazines as if it was the truth, not as a theory.

A theory is a supposition or a system of ideas intended to explain something. Nothing is said in its definition about any supporting evidence.

Evolution explains the origin of man, animals and all of creation leaving out the Creator. By a series of mutations and adaptations nothing has developed into everything in the universe. Teaching about evolution aims to indoctrinate students with the belief that they are evolved animals, and ultimately are, in effect, nothing more than a chance re-arrangements of matter.

The belief that millions or billions of years ago we started out as a one cell piece of slime in the mud is false, not provable and insulting our intelligence.

Our whole educational system in America is saturated by evolution. This is simply fallen sinful man's attempt to justify sinful lifestyle with no accountability to anyone.

Of all the various fields of sciences involved in the theory of evolution, the main foundational kingpin is geology. Geology seems to be one of the key foundations to this belief. It is the science that deals with the earth's physical structure and substance, its history, and the processes that act on it. The conventional model of geology teaches that the earth has been around for millions or perhaps billions of years. By believing the unproven assumptions of most geologists will reflect a flawed and unbiblical model of life. The theory of evolution rests and falls on an old earth allotting millions of years of evolution. When we prove it is only thousands of years old rather than millions, the theory of evolution collapses like a house of cards.

This teaching began in the early 1800's with a flawed belief about the age of the earth, adaptation of a species, and the complexity of the cell. Over the past 150 years we have learned much about the complexity of the cell with the invention of the electron microscope along with changes within a species and the age of the earth. Even with all our current knowledge that men like Darwin and Lyell did not have we are so entrenched in the theory of evolution many cannot or will not look at the evidence for a young earth created by an Intelligent Creator.

The debate over creation and evolution is primarily a dispute between two worldviews, with mutually incompatible underlying assumptions.

If evolution is correct, the Bible obviously is not the literal word of God. And, as a matter of fact, widespread belief in evolution is one of the major reasons why many people do not believe in the Bible.

It is a fallacy to believe that facts speak for themselves—they are always interpreted according to a framework. That is the reason for this academy, to help our children, youth and adults develop a biblical framework.

- Here is the problem; all evidence must be interpreted. Facts don't speak for themselves. Forensic scientists must make multiple assumptions about things they cannot observe. Forensic means methods used for the investigation of a crime scene. What was the original setting? Was the scene contaminated since the event, for instance? One piece of missing evidence could totally change how they reconstruct the past events that led to the present-day evidence.
- I have set up in the corner a mock crime scene and completely preserved all the evidence that was placed in that scene. No one has disturbed the scene. Many times, as a police detective, I have been called out in the middle of the night to many crime scenes. When I arrive, the scene where the crime took place is taped off to preserve any evidence from the crime. It is then collected and analyzed. At a police crime scene you might find bullet casings, finger prints, foot prints, tire prints, blood samples, hair fragments or whatever is left behind. This evidence can be collected and analyzed as long as it has not been altered after the crime. (At this point have an usher go under the tape and begin to sweep the floor and rearrange the chairs.) This is done without me knowing as I continue talking. Now the scene has been contaminated and the evidence altered. It will no longer hold up in court. That is exactly what happened to all the evidence the geologists use to prove the age of the earth. There was a world flood that totally rearranged the entire earth 4,500 years ago which negates the belief of "all things being equal."

It's no accident that the leaders of evolutionary thought were and are ardently opposed to the notion of the Christian God as revealed in the Bible. Stephen Jay Gould and others have shown that Darwin's purpose was to destroy the idea of a divine designer. Richard Dawkins, who later wrote *The God Delusion*, applauds evolution, because he claims that "before Darwin it was impossible to be an intellectually fulfilled atheist".

Many people do not realize that the teaching of evolution propagates an anti-biblical religion.

While Christianity is a religion, and while there is much evidence for the claims of this religion, it still takes a step of faith to become a true believer in the faith.

Evolution is also faith based. The believers in this faith also claim evidence to prove it, but it still takes much faith to follow. Evolutionists do not claim to have faith but claim their belief is that evolution is not just a theory, but is indeed a fact.

The first two tenets of Humanist Manifesto I (1933), signed by many prominent evolutionists are:

1. Religious humanists regard the universe as self-existing and not created.
2. Humanists believe that man is a part of nature and has emerged as a result of a continuous process.

Evolution attempts to explain the origin of life and our planet without God. Their answer to the origin of life is chance happenings, random events and mutations. They believe this is how our universe has developed and it is their explanation of the complexity of our world today.

1. Evolution is not truly science. It can't be repeated, measured and observed. There was no big bang. Every part of the galaxy is fully formed. ** There is no evidence to prove living beings developed gradually over time. In fact it defies the 2nd Law of Thermodynamics that tells us "matter tends toward disorder, not higher order." Entropy is the inevitability of social decline and degeneration, or the measure of energy that is used up. Things are used up, they don't get better. Our universe is winding down or depleting, not enlarging, expanding or increasing. Text books are full of false teaching in schools about evolution (DVD Icons of Evolution 11:05-16:44)
2. Evolution is a hypothesis. The definition of hypothesis is an explanation made on the basis of limited evidence as a starting point for further investigation. There is an abundance of evidence but little to prove evolution. Accepting evolution requires faith in a human theory. Charles Darwin's belief of a simple cell could not have been farther from the truth. That simple cell is fantastically complex—even the simplest self-reproducing organism contains encyclopedic quantities of complex, specific information.
3. Change and development will occur within various species. But there is no evidence on earth or in fossil record of one kind of living thing ever evolving from another kind (Darwin's famous finches do not prove evolution-DVD Icons of Evolution 17:29-19:33; 20:18-21:14).
4. Theistic evolution states God started the evolutionary process. This is not true, nor biblical.
5. Charles Darwin thought the cell was a single simple cell in 1850. In the 1950's, with the invention of the electron microscope, we found the cell is incredibly complex, with hundreds of irreducibly complex motor parts that could not have evolved. (Mouse trap illustration) (Metamorphosis 26:24-34:25 DVD)
6. We have discovered the complexity of the universe and mankind. It is impossible to think all this evolved from nothing to everything without God.

7. A fossil is any preserved remains, impressions, or trace of any once-living thing from a past geological age. If we evolved slowly over millions or billions of years, there should be billions of transitional fossils of living things in-between stages. We have still found none. This fact in and of itself would prove to me the theory of evolution is unprovable and false.
   (DVD Creatures do Change 37:39-43:14)
8. The dating methods used to come up with the theory of our earth being billions of years old are totally unreliable. Radiometric dating methods do not go back billions or millions of years and are totally unreliable. Again, assumptions are made that have been proven to be incorrect. Recently scientists have discovered that rate of decay varies with time. Another factor that is assumed is the starting amount of chemicals in the tested sample. One method of dating a fossil is to date the rocks around it, not the fossil. As we will explain later, this will give a false reading because the entire earth was transformed during and after the global flood (Evolution's Achilles Heels dating system DVD 1:04:42- 1:12:29).

The vast thicknesses of sedimentary rocks around the world are commonly used as evidence for vast age. Sedimentary rocks are formed when solid materials carried by wind and water accumulate in layers and then are compressed by overlying deposits. Sedimentary rocks sometimes contain fossils formed from the parts of organism deposited along with other solid materials. Yes, this vast thickness could be formed by vast amounts of time or, a lot of water over a short period of time. The evidence can be interpreted two different ways according to ones preconceived worldview. The evolutionist needs vast amounts of time to prove their theory. I propose to you the biblical scene; a cataclysmic globe-covering (and fossil-forming) flood would have eroded huge quantities of sediment, and deposited them elsewhere. Many organisms would have been buried very quickly and fossilized during a catastrophic world-wide flood.

If evolution were true, then the Bible and the words of Jesus are false. However, if the Bible's account of Creation is true and Christ's acknowledgment of Adam is true, then evolution is false. The only way we can be absolutely sure of what happened in prehistoric times is for someone who was there and who is trustworthy to tell us what happened. That is exactly what we have in the revealed Word of God.

Our earth is not millions of years old but approximately 6,000 years. There is no empirical proof for millions of years, but without it evolutionists can't make their claim.

The evolutionists tell us the earth is millions of years old because they need this time frame for their belief system. Their belief is that any impossible event will occur if there is enough time.

An example of evolution taught to students is the change in populations of peppered moths in England from a predominantly light, speckled colored variety to a predominantly dark colored variety, due to a progressive darkening of tree trunks on which the moths rest. This occurred as a result of the increase in pollution due to the industrial revolution. It has been characterized by evolutionists as the most astounding example of evolution ever seen by man. Of course, it is not evolution at all. The moths were peppered moths, before the industrial revolution, and they all remain peppered moths, today. The variations that are actually observable today, and which Darwin cited in his book as evidence of evolution, are changes within a species. No one has ever observed one basic kind of plant or animal naturally change into another basic kind.

If evolution were true, then millions of species would have evolved during hundreds of millions of years, because each species developed from some preceding form in turn giving rise to a succeeding form. If true, our natural history museums should contain large quantities of transitional forms. We still have found none.

Evolutionists use a flawed beginning by believing "the present is the key to the past." When in reality the past is key to understanding the present.

Geologists are finding that decay rates may not be the same in the past. However, this may not fit their conventional paradigm of an old earth so we won't look at that possibility. For evolution an old earth is needed so those figures must be flawed.

We have an open system not a closed system so we cannot get dependable decay rates. There is a commitment to millions of years so no one wants to delve into decay rates much faster in the past.

The key difference between a closed system and open system is this: in a closed system, the matter does not exchange with the surrounding but, the energy exchanges with the surrounding. In the open system both matter and energy exchanges with the surrounding.

Darwin was aware of the fact that the fossil record did not produce the evidence his theory predicted, but he hoped future generations would unearth the required evidence. They have not.

It is difficult to understand how anyone, scientifically trained or not, could fail to see the glaring contradiction between the evolutionary theory of the origin of the universe and the Second Law of Thermodynamics, one of the most well established natural laws known in science. This law states that the order, organization, and complexity of an isolated system can never increase, but can only run down and deteriorate with time. There is no exception. Yet evolutionists believe our earth began in a state of chaos and disorder and became more complex over time.

Geologists have established a timetable for their theory of world history and every geology student soon realizes they will need to study and understand the evolution theory laid out in fossil record which is buried in the rocks. This is a horizontal chart with the oldest at the bottom and the youngest at the top. (Display on overhead the geological time chart) The chart (Precambrian-Cambrian-Ordovician-Silurian-Devonian-Mississippion-Pennsylvanian-Permian-Triassic-Jurassic-Cretaceous-Tertiary-Quaternaary) lists the oldest being the Precambrian era 600 million years ago and the youngest Quaternary which is 2.5 million years ago. In the lower rock layers bacteria and jellyfish fossils were found and the most recent 2.5 million years ago evidence of man is found. They show an evolution of development from bacteria to man over millions of years. This is using the well-established theory of Charles Lyell of slow gradual change over time with no catastrophic events taking place. This is called uniformitarianism. If you use this theory of slow change, which we see in the present as a gauge for all of life, then I can see where it would take millions of years for this evolutionary belief. However, we know this earth and all life didn't evolve over long periods of time, so how is the fossil record to be interpreted? Were these rock layers laid over millions of years or over days or even hours? These fossils actually tell of the death of life not the origin of life. Instead of seeing this as evolution of life it should be interpreted as the order of burial during the flood. Looking at the geologist chart the first thing to do is eliminate the ages in the left column because they are simply man made beliefs based on an old earth. As the flood waters rose, there were more and more diversified life forms dying. As the flood waters got higher and higher, there were more fossils of land animals until eventually got the entire land was under water and the larger land animals died.

The Cambrian Explosion of life is used by the evolutionists to prove evolution when in fact it proves the biblical story of the flood.

According to geological time line, the Cambrian era was about 480-540 million years ago. Geological record is the layers of rock in the planets crust. The science of geology is concerned with the age of the rocks which determine the history and formation of earth. This is the timeline of the evolutionary history of life.

Diagram of geological timeline:

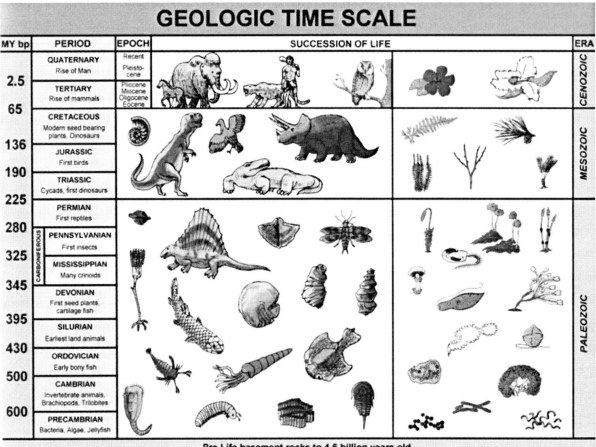

The Bible tells us a much more realistic time line. About 4,500 years ago God destroyed all living things on this planet except those on an ark. For over a year this earth went through a total upheaval. To think we can age earth by the rocks location in the strata they occupy is not correct when we think of the upheaval the entire planet went through. Layers of earth, rocks and fossils were spread in layers and across continents in a very unorthodox fashion; certainly not uniformly.

China's Chengjiang Formation and Canada's Burges Shale are two famous sites revealing the Cambrian explosion—the abrupt appearance of diverse animals deep in the fossil record. The seemingly sudden appearance of so many different kinds of animals at the same time in the fossil record without a similar bumper crop of simpler transitional forms leading up to this is, however, an evolutionary problem. Since vertebrates (having a spine or backbone) are considered an evolutionary advance on invertebrates, (no backbone) the concurrent occurrence of two different vertebrates species so early in the history of life is a problem. If evolution really happened, how could vertebrates have not only evolved so early but also diversified so fast?

In a teaching video, David Attenborough points out that it is "something of a mystery" how soft body parts of dead marine animals in the Chengjiang Formation were preserved at all because bacteria would normally destroy a marine animal like this long before it could be preserved. These animals were buried alive. Because of his predetermined beliefs, he is unable to think outside the box to answer his dilemma.

To make sense of the Cambrian explosion we need to first eliminate the predetermined fossil record of the millions of years labels attached to it. Those dates are assigned by scientists who cling to unverifiable worldview-based assumptions and interpret dating methods accordingly. However, these dating methods have proven to be completely unreliable. We can best understand the significance of fossils like these in the context of the history of life on Earth as understood from the eyewitness account God provided in the Bible. God created all kinds of living things about 6,000 years ago and, as we see from Genesis 1, designed them to vary and reproduce only within their created kinds. Biological observations confirm that living things do just that. They do not evolve into new, more complex kinds of organisms. Thus the fossil record is a record of the order in which many organisms were catastrophically buried, not a timeline revealing the Darwinian order in which living things evolved increasing complexity through natural processes. The lesson here is not about the evolution of life but about catastrophic death of life because of sin. The Precambrian sedimentary rock layers are remnants of pre-flood sedimentary rocks. However, the Cambrian explosion preserves a record of the sudden burial and death of countless organisms that likely lived in the shallow seas adjacent to the pre-flood supercontinent suddenly disrupted by the onset of the global Flood recounted in Genesis 6 through 9. As the lowest fossil-rich sedimentary layers in the geological record, these Cambrian layers represent the first major sedimentary product of the biblical Flood. (Is Genesis History? The Cambrian explosion 42:33-50:03)

There are actually hundreds of dating methods that could be used to attempt an estimate of the earth's age, and the vast majority of them point to a young earth.

Remember, despite the wealth of evidence, it is important to understand that, from the perspective of observational science, no one can prove absolutely how young or old the universe is. Only one dating method is absolutely reliable—a witness who doesn't lie, who has all evidence, and who can reveal to us when the universe began. That is the God of the Bible.

There are over 101 proofs that the world is not over 6,000 years old. Evolutionists will fight this because they need this long time frame for their theory.

Example:

- DNA extracted from bacteria that are supposed to be 425 million years old brings into question that age, because DNA cannot last more than thousands of years.
- The very limited variation in the DNA sequence on the human Y—chromosome around the world is consistent with a recent origin of mankind, thousands not millions of years.
- The ages of the world's oldest living organisms, trees, are consistent with an age of the earth of thousands of years.
- Experiments show that with conditions mimicking natural forces, coal forms quickly; in weeks for brown coal to months for black coal. It does not need millions of years. The same with oil that forms quickly.
- Carbon—14 in coal suggests ages of thousands of years and clearly contradicts ages of millions of years.

- Carbon—14 in oil, in fossil wood, in diamonds all suggests ages of thousands, not billions, of years.
- The amount of salt in the ocean speaks of a young earth. The salty sea benefits man, because the ocean provides many useful minerals for our industries. About 457 million tons of sodium comes into the sea every year and only 122 million tons leave. If the earth were around millions of years the ocean would be salt saturated.
- The small amount of sediment on the sea floor. Every year water and wind erode about 20 billion tons of dirt and rock in the ocean, which settles to the bottom of the ocean. This deposit of sediment is yet only an average thickness of about 1,300 feet. If the earth and sea were millions of years old there should be miles deep of sediment.
- The population of the earth is evidence of a young earth. Population currently doubles every 39 years. If the first humans lived on earth over a million years ago, where are all the trillions of people who should either be alive, or whose buried remains, potentially fossilized, should be found in vast graveyards scattered around the world? Calculating from the world wide flood of Noah in 2348 BC the population should be around 6 billion people and that is what it is.
- Red blood cells, blood vessels, hemoglobin, and collagen have been found in some (un-fossilized) dinosaur bone. But these could not last more than a few thousand years—certainly not for 65 million years, the 'date' for the extinction of the last dinosaurs.
- The earth's magnetic field has been decaying so fast that it couldn't be more than about 10,000 years old.

Here is a list of over 100 reasons our earth is thousands of years old, not millions. Why is this so important? You cannot declare evolution without millions of years for change to take place.

Doesn't it take millions of years to produce coal? Argonne National Laboratory has proven that it doesn't take millions of years to form coal…but instead months. The same principle applies to rocks that some say take millions of years to form.

What about oil or petroleum? Don't they take millions of years to form? Today, turkey and pig slaughterhouse wastes are daily trucked into the world's first bio-refinery, a thermal conversion processing plant in Carthage, Missouri. On peak production days, 500 barrels of high-quality fuel oil better than crude oil are made from 270 tons of turkey guts and 20 tons of pig fat.

Researchers at the Pacific Northwest National Laboratory in Washington State have pioneered a new technology that makes diesel fuel from algae—and their cutting-edge machine produces the fuel in minutes…Simply heat pea-green algal soup to 662degrees at 3,000 psi for almost 60 minutes.

Even sewage sludge is being used to make oil in Australia. The same is true with gems, petrified fossils and so much more we have been told takes millions of years to produce.

The global flood changed the entire earth… mountains, valleys, Grand Canyon, and continents.

Evolution is not true and is an attempt by man to eliminate God as Creator.

By quoting a leading professor, biologist and scientist D.M.S. Watson, will explain the major tenant or purpose of evolution, "Evolution is a theory universally accepted not because it can be proven by logically coherent evidence to be true, but because the only alternative, special creation, is clearly incredible".

Many of our schools have become training grounds for teaching socialism and rebellion. Our youth do not believe there is any objective truth. Our nation's earliest schools were home schools and private Christian schools, and these produced the highest percentage of both literacy and morality in any nation's history. There is no biblical warrant for government-controlled schools. Almost the same can be said of secularized religious schools. Concerned parents should not entrust their children's spiritual and educational health to them. Parents need to have some real heartfelt thinking about who will mold their children's character and minds.

Kingdom Quiz (The Great Deception-The Theory of Evolution)

1. How many transitional fossils do museums display today?

2. Is evolution true science? Why?

3. Is the cell really a simple cell?

4. What is a fossil?

5. Why do evolutionists tell us the earth is millions of years old?

6. What is the Second Law of Thermodynamics?

7. Why does the above law disprove evolution?

8. Give one example that proves the earth is young, not old?

9. What event changed the structure of the entire earth?

God's Design for the Family

Before going into God's design for the family, we need to understand the basis of this belief and how it differs from the conventional view of the family that we are seeing in our country today.

God established the first family and wrote the definition in the Bible, His manual, for every couple to follow. Looking at our progressive culture today, we will find a second and very different model.

There are two models of the family to choose from:

a. The biblical model. It is the definition God has given the church to follow.

b. The secular model. This is a progressively changing model which varies as the culture changes.

One model ends in fulfillment, legacy and rewards, the other ends with hurt, regret and judgment.

The danger is when the church or Christians begin to follow the world's model. God tells believers not to love or follow the ways of the ever changing world but to follow His never changing pattern (I John 2:15; James 4:4; Ezekiel 11:12).

God's plan for marriage and family is clearly stated in Genesis 1:27-28; 2:20-24; Matthew 19:4-5. God made Eve out of Adam's own flesh, the perfect helpmate for Adam, (Genesis 2:24) to be his wife. This husband and wife are to be the foundation of the family. The marriage of man and woman is oriented toward producing and raising children, if God so blesses (Genesis 1:28; Malachi 2:15). The world was populated by Adam and Eve. God made them biologically different to desire one another for intimacy and procreation. A woman has breasts to be able to feed her baby. Each partner was designed and formed specifically for the purpose of procreating. God wanted to fill the earth with people who would love and serve Him. God made the two not only biologically different but physically and emotionally different. He even gave them a hierarchy in marriage for the purpose of order and protection (Ephesians 5:22-33).

God has not only formed male and female, but He also has designed marriage and the family to accomplish His overall purposes.

God's plan for marriage is to reflect His image. "So God created man in His own image, in the image of God He created Him; male and female He created them." (Genesis 1:26-27).

The family serves a crucial role in God's kingdom plans on earth. Christ uses the family to illustrate His relationship with the church (Ephesians 5:22-33). The influence of a good father and mother balances a child and teaches the young to be both strong and gentle. From a mother, a child learns the nature of mercy. From a father, a child learns the importance of justice, the need to fulfill obligations and to perform one's duties or suffer the consequences. There are many families that are broken up and lack a father in the home, but that does not change God's original plan.

Satan, our enemy has tried to destroy God's plan since the beginning.

Why is marriage so important? Because it is God's plan for a setting to raise a healthy God honoring family.

Our culture has changed and many couples choose to live together before marriage or just live together and eliminate the costly wedding. Cohabitation (living together) before marriage has become widely accepted. What does God say about this practice? "Marriage is honorable among all, and the bed undefiled; but fornicators and adulterers God will judge." Hebrews 13:4. Living together before marriage is clearly described here as fornication and adultery.

Throughout the world, living together before marriage is becoming more and more common. Just a few generations ago this practice was virtually inconceivable. However, in recent years we have seen a spiritual decay, both in individuals and in churches all over the world, where cohabitation and homosexual unions are becoming more and more acceptable. We find that as sin becomes more widespread and widely accepted, resistance decreases, even among those who call themselves Christians. It is when the light from heaven is extinguished that people with unclean spirits can find peace in the congregation. Such an assembly is without power and blessing and the seeking soul cannot find help.

If a person is a follower of the crowd, i.e., the majority, they might not see the grave error of living together before marriage because everyone is doing it. However, Jesus did tell us the majority will not choose to follow Him (Matthew 7:13-14) so we should not be surprised.

Scripture is quite clear (Acts 15:19-20; 15:28-29) one cannot live for God as a disciple of Christ, while at the same time living together before marriage—living in adultery. There are countless reasons not to live together before marriage besides obeying God:

- There is a higher rate of divorce for those who live together before marriage.
- Marriage changes you for the better. You do not know the other person truly before marriage. Now with the commitment of marriage you can grow and change together.
- Marriage grows intimacy at all levels. Living together without marriage separates sex from covenant. Sex is meant to be a reaffirmation of the covenant that has joined two people in marriage. Living together without the bonds of a covenant means that even as we are giving ourselves physically to another person, we are withholding our full commitment to that person. In effect, we are promising to give our bodies, but not our lives.
- Marriage is God's design. Living together in a sexually intimate relationship outside of marriage is displeasing to God (I Corinthians 6:18; Galatians 5:19; Ephesians 5:3; I Thessalonians 4:3).

Do not buy into the lies of our culture girls. Lies like:

- Lie #1 No guy will like you unless you move in with him. If a guy expects you to move in with him, he is not respecting God or you. A Christian man of integrity will neither expect nor request this of you.
- Lie #2 You will change him for the better if you live together. He's not going to magically improve when you share the same address. Why would he need to impress you if he's already got you where he wants you?
- Lie #3 Moving in with him will make him pop the question. Actually, it will probably delay a proposal, because he's getting all the benefits of a wife without the commitment or responsibility. In fact, statistics claim that cohabitation lessens your chances of ever marrying him by 50 percent. Have you ever heard the expression, "Why buy the cow if the milk is free?"

- Lie #4 You won't know if you're compatible unless you live together. Cohabitation is a smart way to test out whether you would survive marriage. Treating cohabitation as marriage "insurance" is a very unstable foundation, one built partially on fear and partially on selfishness. The truth is, you can't practice marriage. Marriage is a permanent commitment.

Statistics prove that cohabitation is not a healthy way for a relationship to progress; in fact, cohabitation can decrease your chances of getting married and couples who do marry after cohabitating are more likely to divorce.

When sexual activity is practiced outside of marriage, abortions increase. Abortion is killing a baby in the mother's belly. A doctor takes a sharp instrument and cuts the baby into pieces then removes it from the mother's stomach. Sometimes the baby is alive so they kill it on the way out. Abortion is a sin and murder. Women fight that statement because they say it is their body and they can do whatever they want with their body. Life begins at conception. When the man's sperm unites with the woman's egg life begins.

We live in a culture that seems to be attempting to redefine everything that God has ordained. This is especially true in issues of family, marriage and gender.

Our culture is not just becoming more accepting of a new definition of family but is aggressively pushing this redefinition as good, healthy, and enlightened. But rejecting God's original design is the opposite of good, healthy, or enlightened.

All throughout Scripture we see examples of people who thought that they knew better than God, and every time it led to judgment and tragedy.

In the Western world, a large part of this battle is being fought over the definition of family. Our culture is increasingly trying to redefine family to be whatever people want it to be. TV shows, commercials, and other pop culture mediums often portray families as made up of two fathers or two mothers.

Throughout the Bible and throughout history we see that the family consists of one man, one woman and then children. I remember hearing how to build a family when I was a little boy:

Donnie and Bonnie sitting in a tree

K-I-S-S-I-N-G

First comes love

Then comes marriage

Then comes Bonnie with a baby carriage!

Homosexuality is not God's plan. Homosexuals are not to be hated. The church should never hate people. We can hate sin but not the sinner.

Our culture tells us if we don't go along with the world's view of a "couple" we are prejudiced. There are attempts to make Christians look like the bad guys.

Homosexuality is a sin and has always been a sin as far back in times as Sodom and Gomorrah. God destroyed these two cities not just because of homosexuality but because they were destroying God's plan for the family.

This is not about liking or not liking someone. Many homosexual men and women are very sensitive, caring people. It is about violating God's plan and prototype for the family to raise children.

An example of God's displeasure in this lifestyle is found in the fact that homosexuals average life span is 30 years less than the average population. Suicide is the 2nd leading cause of death among young people ages 10 to 24. LGB youth seriously contemplate suicide at almost three times the rate of heterosexual youth. LGT youth are almost five times as likely to have attempted suicide compared to heterosexual youth.

We don't hate homosexuals nor does God, but it is perversion and not natural (Romans 1:18-28). There are many scriptures that condemn homosexuality (Leviticus 18:22; I Corinthians 6:9-11; Genesis 19; I Timothy 1:8-11; Jude 7-8; Ezekiel 16:46-50). These are clear passages; however, some homosexual advocates have been remarkably effective in selling their warped interpretations of passages in Scripture that address homosexuality. I know that many of your friends may be homosexual or bi-sexual and they may be very kind and creative people. No one is saying they are not nice or not creative and kind. Sex is God's idea. It is for procreation and enjoyment within the marriage of one man and one woman. Sex before marriage is wrong and is sin. Boys and girls should not be involved in sexual activity until marriage. That is God's plan.

I am well aware the homosexual lifestyle is being accepted by more people each year. A Pew Research Center survey in 2014 found 54 percent of U.S. Christians say homosexuality should be accepted by society. This is up 10 percentage points from a similar survey from 2007. Young Christians led the shift.

The majority of heterosexuals believe homosexuals want to love and be loved just like them so they advocate letting them practice their love and get married just like they do. They declare that homosexuals have a right to be happy just like heterosexuals. However, no one is talking about love or happiness; we are talking about right and wrong. While live and let live is commendable, many have no idea that God is the author of sex and marriage so they have no right to authorize any change in His plan.

The reason, then, that the Bible opposes the homosexual lifestyle is that it violates God's design for marriage and family. Two people of the same gender do not complement one another as husband and wife do. Their union cannot produce children.

In His great wisdom, God has created the human family as the first school to form the minds, hearts, souls, and conscience of children. In God's plan, a child needs a mother and a father.

It simply boils down to whom do we follow, and whom do we want to please. Do we follow the majority or the chosen few? The road is broad that leads to destruction and many are on it, but the road to life is narrow and difficult to follow and few are on it (Matthew 7:13-14).

Homosexuals are not to be rejected, but loved and accepted. It is their lifestyle that is to be rejected.

Even now that same-sex marriage has become widely accepted in many countries, Christians cannot surrender. We must continue to lovingly and graciously stand for the truth. Also, if we want to be effective, we must learn to articulate the reasons why gay marriage not only violates God's moral standard, but actually harms society.

Holding the line on this belief may come at a price, such as rejection or persecution. So each person will need to have a firm conviction of their beliefs and why they believe as they do.

What is the harm of accepting same sex marriage?

1. Same-sex marriage debases true marriage, and thereby weakens society. Once the definition of marriage is separated from the Creator's design, it becomes so flexible that it begins to lose any significant meaning. Many homosexual activists have admitted that their real goal is to destroy the institution of marriage altogether. Healthy societies are built on healthy families. The further we move away from the biblical teaching on marriage, the more we'll have broken homes. The reason is because other arrangements simply do not work as well as God's design. Weakening of marriage will place a burden on society as a whole, because others will have to step in with time, energy, and money to try to repair the damage.

2. Same-sex marriage harms children. What's wrong with the same-sex couples producing children through a surrogate, or adopting children? The fact that many children require adoption means they are already in a less-than-ideal situation. The ideal is that children would be raised by their own parents. Children long for and tend to be healthier when raised by their biological mother and father. Adoption by a same-sex couple would give children additional difficulties to overcome instead of giving them the best chance for success.

3. Same-sex marriage undermines religious freedom. It should not be surprising that, once gay marriage was declared legal, those who oppose it are seen as enemies of the law. That is why, especially since the Supreme Court ruling on same-sex marriage, those with moral and religious objections to same-sex marriage are increasingly being persecuted for simply following their deeply held religious convictions. Religious adoption agencies are being forced to close if they will not place children into same-sex households. Christian schools are being threatened with loss of funding and accreditation if they do not allow their students to actively engage in homosexual practices.

Clearly, gay marriage advocates want more than the freedom to do as they please. The movement includes many bullies who want to force everyone to either join them or be destroyed.

Homosexuals, and those who advocate that sin, are fundamentally committed to overturning the lordship of Christ in this world. As we interact with homosexuals and their sympathizers, we must be loving but continue to affirm the Bible's condemnation of the sin. We are not trying to bring damnation on the head of homosexuals; we are trying to bring conviction so that they can turn away from the sin and embrace the only hope of salvation.

Another recent trend, especially with youth, is bisexuality. Nowhere in the Bible is bisexuality mentioned. However, it is clear from the Bible's view of homosexuality that bisexuality would also be considered sinful. Leviticus 18:22 declares having sexual relations with the same sex to be an abomination. Romans 1:26-27 condemns sexual relations between the same sex as abandoning what is natural. I Corinthians 6:9 states that homosexual offenders will not inherit the kingdom of God. These truths apply equally to bisexuals and to homosexuals.

Satan always hates what God loves. God loves the family. He established the marriage of a man and woman as a physical representation of His love for the church and the church's love for Him. God effectively says, "You want to know how much I love my people? Look at the way that Christian man loves his wife. You want to know how much My people love Me? Look at the way that Christian woman loves her husband. This is My model. This is

My example for all of you to observe." Therefore it should come as no surprise that the devil would try to undermine the family.

Kingdom Quiz (God's Design for the Family)

1. Who was the very first couple in the world?

2. God used the family to illustrate His relationship with His _____.

3. Who is trying to destroy God's plan for the family?

4. Who created sex?

5. Our culture is attempting to redefine the _____.

6. What is abortion?

7. When does life begin?

The Foundation of America

To find the history of our country we will need to do some research because many modern text books and other historical documents describing our beginnings have been altered and leave out key elements of our beginnings. Just a brief history lesson should answer any questions and concerns about our Christian foundation because many do not understand the ground work of this wonderful nation. Nor do they realize this form of government, where the people elect their leaders, is an experiment never before tried. Our founders were men and women who believed in God and wanted to obey Him. The Pilgrims came to this country to expand God's Kingdom. Before leaving the ship on September 6, 1620 they wrote The Mayflower Compact as their guiding principles. The purpose of the voyage was stated in that compact, "Having undertaken for the Glory of God, **and advancement of the Christian faith,** and the honor of our king and country, a voyage to plant the first colony in the northern part of Virginia." One hundred and fifty years later the first president of this country, George Washington stated, **"It is the duty of all nations to acknowledge the providence of almighty God, to obey His will, to be grateful for His benefits, and humbly to implore His protection and favor."** In his farewell address in 1796, Washington said**, "Of all the dispositions and habits which lead to political prosperity, religion and morality are indispensable supports."** He knew that without religion and morality, America was doomed. Historians believe that America wouldn't even exist without the leadership of George Washington. God was with him, the first great American warrior.

The Bible was used in the schools to teach reading for more than two hundred years. The New England Primer, introduced in Boston the year 1690 by Benjamin Harris, was the first textbook printed in America. For over two centuries after its introduction, it was the beginning textbook for students, and lasted well into the twentieth century (1930 last printing). It continued to be a principal text in all types of American schools: public, private, semi-private, home, and parochial. The core of the Primer was Bible stories, not "Dick and Jane." The New England Primer's rhyming alphabet, alphabet of lessons for youth, Bible questions and short catechism was Bible based.

Our second president, John Adams stated, **"We have no government armed with power capable of contending with human passions unbridled by morality and religion. Our Constitution was made only for a moral and religious people. It is wholly inadequate to the government of any other."** Is it any wonder why so many liberal progressive anti- god leaders today want to write a different constitution? The present one does not fit in a liberal progressive society and our founders told us that.

Our third president, Thomas Jefferson stated**, "Can the liberties of a nation be thought secure when we have removed their only firm basis, a conviction in the minds of the people that these liberties are of the gift of God? That they are not to be violated but with His wrath? Indeed I tremble for my country when I reflect that God is just; that His justice cannot sleep forever."**

Benjamin Franklin stated, **"I've lived, sir, a long time, and the longer I live, the more convincing proofs I see of this truth: That God governs in the affairs of men. If a sparrow cannot fall to the ground without His notice, is it probable that an empire can rise without His aid? We've been assured in the sacred writings that unless the Lord builds the house, they labor in vain who build it. I firmly believe this, and I also believe that without His concurring aid, we shall succeed in this political building no better than the builders of Babel."**

The first chief justice of the Supreme Court, John Jay stated, **"The Bible is the best of all books, for it is the word of God and teaches us the way to be happy in this world and in the next. Continue therefore to read it and to regulate your life by its precepts."**

"We are a Christian people…not because the law demands it, not to gain exclusive benefits or to avoid legal disabilities, but from choice and education; and in a land thus universally Christian, what is to be expected, what desired, but that we shall pay due regard to Christianity?" Senate Judiciary Committee Report, January 19, 1853.

"At the time of the adoption of the Constitution and the amendments, the universal sentiment was that Christianity should be encouraged…In this age there can be no substitute for Christianity… That was the religion of the founders of the republic and they expected it to remain the religion of their descendants." House Judiciary Committee Report, March 27, 1854.

French historian Aleis de Tocqueville, after studying American history wrote, **"Religion and morality were indispensable to the maintenance of the American republic. While the constitutional law of liberty allowed Americans complete freedom to do as they please, religion prevented them from doing that which is immoral and unjust."**

Those quotes alone should answer the question of the founder's beliefs and intent in pioneering this country.

The Christian Culture at Risk

In today's ever changing culture, historical revisionists will often leave out the Christian foundational principles and beliefs in their writings, as well as our text books. As this happens our young people are not taught true and complete history, as we know it, as a nation. Our children are taught what the political and educational leaders want them to know about our history, often leaving out what doesn't conform to their agendas. In today's culture, Christianity is not popular as it seems so exclusive.

Public school texts paint rosy pictures of other cultures while emphasizing the negative aspects of Western societies. To suit politically correct sensibilities, textbook writers and publishers are rewriting what American students learn. Universities have installed "speech codes" to punish any student or faculty member who does not abide by the new ethics of equality for "disadvantaged" groups based on their sex, race, sexual orientation, or disability. As the latest "disadvantaged or marginalized" minority group in the line-up of victims looking for liberation from their oppressors, homosexuals now assert their "rights" for acceptance into the American mainstream. One of the top priorities of the homosexual movement is to force a 'redefinition' of the American family away from the traditional husband-wife-children model." I am reminded of this at every wedding I perform as the bride and groom sign their marriage license. No longer does it read bride and groom, but spouse and spouse.

Kingdom Quiz (The Foundation of America)

1. Who were the first settlers in America?

2. What was the name of their agreement they signed before leaving their ship?

3. What was one of their primary reasons for coming to America?

4. Who said, "Without religion and morality America is doomed."

5. What was the name of the first book used in schools to teach reading?

6. Who said, "Our constitution was made only for a moral; and religious people. It is wholly inadequate to the government of any other."

7. Is today's culture becoming more religious or less?

8. What does "historical revision" mean?

Who is Jesus

It is generally accepted that Jesus was truly a man who walked on the earth in Israel 2000 years ago. Only a fool would deny this clear and provable fact. The debate begins when the full identity of Jesus is discussed.

The predominant theme of the whole Bible is the Person and work of Jesus Christ. He is God. He became a human being, died by crucifixion, and was buried. He rose again from the dead. He is the only, all-sufficient Savior of the world. He will come again to this earth.

All this is provable in a court of law today, using the evidence we have.

The name Jesus is the Greek version of the Hebrew Y'shua "YHWH" which means "The Lord, God saves"

Jesus was His official name. Christ, however, was not his last name. It was simply a title for Him meaning "the Anointed One", "Messiah" or "Savior".

**Why do we need a Savior? Because all have sinned and the wages of sin is spiritual death or separation from God and missing heaven (Romans 3:23). Jesus died for our sins. We just need to believe this and ask Him to forgive us, and then ask Him into our lives.

Jesus Christ is God not just, a great teacher, or prophet but God Himself. Jesus has to be God because if He is not God, His death would not have been sufficient to pay the penalty for the sins of the whole world (I John 2:2).

a. He was pre-existent with the Father (John 1:2-3; 17:5 and Colossians 1:17).
b. He is the Son of God (John 6:69NKJ).
c. He is not only the Son of God but God in the flesh. He said, "If you have seen Me you have seen the Father (John 14:9-10).
d. He was sinless, as only God can be (2 Corinthians 5:21 KJV).
e. He never married nor had any children as some false teachers claim.
f. He forgives sin, as only God is able (John 8:11).
g. He performed many miracles and healings.

Jesus Christ became man (John 1:14KJV). He was totally God and totally man, but sat aside His deity (deity means He is God) and lived and died out of His humanity.

a. His miraculous birth was prophesied 800 years before His coming (Isaiah 7:14KJV).
b. Jesus demonstrated human characteristics: He become tired, thirsty, hungry, showed feelings, wept, was tempted yet never sinned.

Jesus Accomplished the Works of His Father:

a. He died on the cross (John 12:27; Isaiah 53:3-8).
b. He was resurrected from the dead: This is unique and fundamental to Christianity (John 20:1-10). Jesus predicted it.

The Results of His work:

    a. He ascended to His Father (Luke 24:49-53).

    b. He is our eternal Mediator (Mediator means He represents us when our accuser, the devil, accuses us, Jesus stands up for us) (I Timothy 2:5).

    c. He is our Savior (Matthew 1:21).

The Consummation of His Work:

    a. He shall return again to this earth (Acts 1:11). He will judge the world (Matthew 24:27-30).

    b. Believers in Christ shall be bodily resurrected to begin a new, undying life (I Thessalonians 4:17-18).

    c. He will reign as King of kings and Lord of lords over His new creation (2 Peter 3:10-13).

The source of salvation and eternal life is only in Jesus (John 6:40).

Jesus brought the kingdom of God to earth (Mark 1:15; Matthew 12:28).

*** Jesus is the only way to the Father (John 14:6; John 10:1,7,9; Luke 10:22; Matthew 7:13-14). There is no other way to get to heaven. No other religions or beliefs have paid for our sins.

He is not one of several ways, but the one and only way to have our sins forgiven and see God.

To become a Christian today is to be born-again. Jesus told Nicodemus this and this remains the same today. Are you born-again?

Why do I need to be born-again?

John 3:16 tells us Jesus loves the world and that means you!

Kingdom Quiz (Who Jesus Is)

1. Was Jesus a man or was He God?

2. How do we become a Christian?

3. Does Jesus have a last name?

4. Is Jesus the only way to get to heaven?

5. What is the theme of the whole Bible?

6. Was Jesus totally sinless?

7. Why did Jesus die?

8. Does Jesus love you?

The World Wide Flood of Noah's Day

The Bible tells us why and how the entire earth was destroyed by a worldwide flood and how God saved Noah and his family (Genesis 6-9). The ark finally rested on Mount Ararat.

During the Flood, as huge tidal waves pulsed back and forth over the existing continents, different types of sediment and ecosystems were picked up, carried, then deposited in massive layers on top of each other. The presence of marine fossils on the continents, the sudden appearance of complex fossils in the lowest Cambrian layers, the widespread extent of fossilization, and the pattern of footprints below body fossils, all point to the record in Genesis where God said He was going to wipe out a violent earth with a global flood.

There is an exact replica of Noah's ark in Kentucky today. If you visit the ark you will see, on the first floor, a plaque indicating those who helped fund this project and Old Town Christian Outreach Center is one of those who helped build this ark.

Has anyone ever seen the original ark? Could it still be visible after 4,500 years?

- Jacob Chuchian, who lived on the south side of Ararat, allegedly saw the Ark a number of times in the late 1800's and early 1900's. His son was interviewed in 1975 by Ark researcher Stuart Brassie. A record of the interview is found in the following book, Balsiger, David W., and Charles E. Sellier. Miraculous Message From Noah's Flood to the End Times. Alachus, Fl: Bridge-Logos, 2008:219.
- George Hagopian: 1908 & 1910. As a young Armenian, whose grandfather was a minister in an Armenian Orthodox Church in Van, he had heard many times of Noah's Ark high atop Ararat. In fact, at that time, many locals, especially shepherds, claimed to know exactly where it was located on the mountain. When George was ten years old, old enough to handle such a hike, his uncle decided to take him up the mountain to see it for himself. George saw the Ark in about 1908 and then again in about 1910. Details are found in the book written by John Morris, The Ark on Ararat. Nashville: Creation-life Publishers, 1976: 68.
- The Russian expedition: 1916-1917. Colonel Alexander Koor was an officer in the Russian White Army in 1915. Though he was not on the expedition to the Ark, he had knowledge of it. He recounts how Russian pilots spotted the Ark, how Czar Nicholas II commissioned the expeditions with two groups of men, one with 50, one with 100. He mentions that the Ark was measured and photographed. He states that the official records were lost during the Bolshevik Revolution. Colonel Koor communicated with Ark researcher Eryl Cummings in 1946, and gave great details which are on record. An American, by the name of Alvin Holderbecker reported that his aunt, who did housekeeping for Czar Nicholas II, heard of the expedition in detail; it is also recorded.
- Russian resident Galina Lochadkina was interviewed in 2011 by Panaghia Rush. Galina recounts her grandfather picking her up from school when she was young. Her grandfather asked her what she had learned at school that day. She told him they discussed Mount Ararat and Noah's Ark.

  Though he had never said a word before, he proceeded to tell her about the Russian expedition to Mount Ararat. Her grandfather, Batov Fedor Frolovich, was in the Russian White Army. He was on the expedition to the Ark in 1917. He told her in great detail all about the Ark (Galina Loshadkina, "Noah's Ark Expedition" Science and Religion, Translated from Russian by the Translation Agency of Alberta.   1994: No. 7.

- Sergeant Ed Davis, U.S. Army Corps of Engineers in 1943 was stationed in Iran. One day he was working out of a quarry in sight of Ararat. One of his truck drivers was a local lad with a long family history of hiking up the mountain. It is said that Davis did a favor for a local village which brought him, as a foreigner, into favor with locals. He was taken up to the Ark by locals. He gives great detail of the structure, size, number of rooms and their sizes etc. as he observes. His story was in such detail it was hard to believe for the skeptic so he even took and passed a polygraph test. (B.J. Corbin, The Explorers of Ararat and The Search for Noah's Ark along with Balsinger, David W., and Charles E. Sellier, Miraculous Message From Noah's Flood to The End Times, Logos press p. 283-284).

- U.S. Air Force Corporal Lester Walton, in 1945-1946 was stationed at Wright Patterson Air Force Base in Ohio during the Second World War. One of his assignments was the testing of a new high altitude camera produced by the Fairchild Camera and Instrument Corporation founded by Sherman Fairchild, a company that spearheaded a lot of research and development during World War II. During the winter months, between 1945 and 1946, Lester Walton, with others, was invited into a theatre to watch black and white footage taken a few months earlier with the new camera. They watched footage taken by a squadron of B-24's which were flying from Africa to Eastern Europe. They flew over Mt. Ararat, and pictures were taken along the way from an altitude of about 20,000 feet. Apparently, they inadvertently snapped some shots of Noah's Ark. It was on the north side of the mountain, near a large canyon. The Corporal recounted that a number of those who saw the footage believed this to be the Ark of Noah (The Explorers of Ararat and The Search for Noah's Ark p.408-409).

- In an unlogged mission from his superiors, on June of 1974, U.S. Navy Lieutenant JG Al Shappell and a navy pilot boarded an F-4 jet fitted with cameras to document a possible Soviet threat on Mount Ararat. Amazingly, the dark box-shaped object was apparently of man-made origin, but it turned out not to be a military threat. This mission was a highly secret reconnaissance trip over Mount Ararat to photograph something that they thought might be a Soviet-made defense installation or radar station with a black tarp over it. A satellite photo of a foreign object toward the summit of Ararat was their mission. The film was top secret and turned over to the Air Force. Lieutenant Shappell said, "I am not sure what they did with it, but I can tell you what I saw with my own eyes. It looked like a boat-like object, definitely manmade. It also appeared as though it did not belong on the mountain. It was just totally out of place." He then gives dimensions and positions (Ibid p. 450-451).

- In 1985, Elfred Lee, along with astronaut Colonel James Irwin, and Ark researcher Eryl Cummings, met with U.S. General Ralph E. Haven. According to his U.S. Air Force biography, he was the "commander of the United States Logistic Group, Ankara Air Station, Turkey. In this position he was the commander of U.S. Air Force personnel in Turkey and responsible for conducting exercises and the logistics support of all United States armed forces in that country. Elfred Lee showed him the drawing he had done based on the eyewitness accounts of Ed Davis and George Hagopian. This photographic copy was produced by Sun Classic Pictures in 1976 to promote a documentary entitled In Search of Noah's Ark. When General Havens saw the re-creation of the Ark that George Hagopian described he said, "We've seen that. We have photos of that. Our pilots have photographed that very object. It looks just like that. It is on a ledge. In fact, I was shown two slides of this object at Fort Leavenworth in a presentation for people assigned to Turkey" (Ibid 458-459).

There are literally dozens and dozens of eyewitnesses who have claimed to have seen the Ark of Noah on Mount Ararat in Turkey over the last 150 years. Even though most of these people did not know each other, their testimonies have major points of similarity with each other and the biblical description of the Ark as a chest-shaped or box-shaped object, having the dimensions of about 500 feet by 83 foot by 50 foot.

There are over 300 Flood legends worldwide. These stories are recorded in Native American history, Aboriginal Australian cultures, Aztec legends of the Flood, Hawaiian Legend of the Flood, Chinese Legend of the Flood, Miao Legend of the Flood, Tanzania Legend of the Flood, Celtic Legends, Babylonia Legends, Ireland, Israel, Germany, Scandinavia, Central Asia, India, Alaska, Mexico Guyana, along with other cultures that record a Global Flood (not regional but global). These Flood legends are an excellent confirmation of what we expected to find in a biblical worldview. Flood legends are also useful in witnessing the true history of the world as a foundation to the Gospel.

As Noah's descendants scattered across the globe (Genesis 11:1-9), these people took their history of the flood with them and it varied and deviated due to the effects of sin.

Second to creation, the flood of Noah is the most significant event this earth has ever experienced.

To reject this event or believe it was simply a regional flood puts a person or even a scientist at a distinct disadvantage as they will be unable to understand history and earth science correctly. (DVD "It's A Great Time to be a Christian" 40:00-45:42)

Think about the local flooding's and the devastation they can do. Then think about a global flood that leaves flood damage for a year.

The information I am about to share with you regarding the flood and the Ice Age comes first and foremost from the Bible. Also reliable information from various men in their fields of science has been used such as,

Geologists, paleontologists, taphonomists, microbiologists, marine biologists, biologists, astronomers, archeologists, atmospheric scientists.

Geology is the science of the earth's physical structure and substances, its history, and the processes that act upon it.

The flood described in Scripture was so massive that the very crust of the earth broke apart (Genesis 7:11-12).

The evidence for a worldwide flood is everywhere and is a game changer for accurate understanding of geology.

A major premise in geology is the statement "all things being equal" or the teaching of "uniformitarians." This is the theory that purports that the remote geological past is not different from those observed now.

Therefore, the theory of uniformity of the earth is flawed as the whole earth was altered 4,359 years ago, (Genesis 7:11) during and after the flood. Therefore, geology as taught in most schools and colleges by using this flawed geological timetable is flawed and in grave error.

Because they don't believe in the worldwide flood, scientists came up with a theory that states it took millions of years to form the layers of the earth when it actually happened in days, not years. The flood was much more than a heavy rain for 40 days and nights. The earth's crust broke open and spewed lava; there were volcanos, tsunamis, earth quakes and the earth broke up into seven continents.

Because many scientists don't understand the impact of the worldwide flood, the same is true for the study of archaeology. Archaeology is the study of human history and prehistory through the excavation of sites and the analysis of artifacts and other physical remains.

But why did God destroy the people He Created? (Genesis 6:5,8)

Every human being on the face of the earth had turned after the wickedness in their own hearts, except Noah and his family.

Let's review some correct biblical dating timelines.

The date of creation   4004B.C.

The date of the flood 2348 B.C.

The number of years since the flood, approximately 4,360

What was the population of the earth at the time of Noah's Flood?

Several factors must be considered to help determine the population before the flood. First, man's life span ranged up to 900 years. For instance when Adam died there were seven generations of his own offspring on the earth. Well over 120,000 in his family.

Now from Adam to Noah was over 1,656 years and a conservative estimate of growth would place the population at the time of the flood at least 7 billion people. That is equal to our world today.

When I first read this, it was hard to believe. Let's briefly look at the figures that bring us to those numbers.

Seven parameters determine how fast population grows. They are:

- The number of years between creation and the flood
- The average mother's age when her first child is born
- The average number of children per family
- The number of years between children
- The percent infertile or who never marry
- The average age of death
- The maximum sustainable population of earth

Using information in Genesis five, logic, and information from modern society we can figure out approximates.

Years from Creation to flood...1656

Age of mothers when first child is born, likely older since they lived so long-60

Average number of children per family conservative -6-

Years between children -5-

Percent infertile or never married (Likely small since few genetic problems) -2-

Average age of death (most men listed lived over 900 years) 900

Maximum sustainable population (in billions) 30

A reasonable, yet low estimate would produce a population of nearly 15 billion people at the time of the flood. It was huge. Best estimates would put it at more than the population of the world today.

Another source explains Adam and Eve had seven children. Using 5-8 children per family, the population falls within a range of 2 billion to 11.5 billion (over the range of 16-22 generations). It is interesting that today's population of approximately 6 billion falls within this category.

I want you to see and understand the purpose of the flood and the reality of it, along with all the evidence we find to support it.

The account of Noah and the Ark is one of the most widely known events in the history of mankind, yet by many thought of as a fairy tale.

Chapter 6 of Genesis gives us the answers to our questions.

How large was the Ark

The Bible tells us it was (Genesis 6:15) 510 feet long, 85 feet wide and 51 feet high. The proportions are like that of a modern cargo ship. The ark was about the size of 522 railroad cars. Only 188 railroad cars would be required to hold a pair of each of the 1,500 species of animals and flying creatures, according to Dr. John Morris of the Institute of Creation Research.

How could Noah build the Ark?

The physical strength and mental processes of men in Noah's day was at least as great (quite likely even superior) to our own. Adam's descendants were making complex musical instruments, forging metal and building cities—their tools, machines, and techniques were not primitive.

How could Noah round up so many animals?

Genesis 6:20 tells us God brought them to the Ark, similar to migrating birds today. The animals were not afraid of Noah because no one killed them for food, all mankind and most animals were vegetarians.

Were dinosaurs on Noah's Ark?

Dinosaurs died out 60 million years before man; that is what we are taught in school. Near Glen Rose, Texas, in the bed of the Paluxy River, are fossilized dinosaur tracts. That is not surprising, because dinosaur tracks are found in many places throughout the world. What is surprising is that human footprints are fossilized in the same rock stratum, with some of the human tracts fossilized as actually stepping into the dinosaur tracts. So here is the fact, preserved in stone, man existed with dinosaurs. Therefore, man did not evolve from dinosaurs!

The history of God's creation (Genesis 1 and 2) tells us that all the land-dwelling creatures were made on day six of creation week—the same day God made Adam and Eve. Most dinosaurs were not very large at all. Some were the size of a chicken. Most scientists agree that the average size of a dinosaur is actually the size of a large sheep or bison.

Yes there were dinosaurs on the Ark. Like all the animals, they would be the young. Therefore when they got off the Ark, they would have a full lifetime to reproduce after its kind.

Job chapter 40 talks of "behemoth" as dinosaur as well as many legends of dragons after the flood. Marco Polo encountered dinosaurs in the year 1272.

We also find many dinosaurs that were trapped and fossilized in flood sediment.

The second week of class one of our youth asked me about the dinosaurs. He said he was told a meteor fell to the earth and killed all the dinosaurs 65 million years ago. The meteor story first started about 1980. Some scientists teach that a huge meteor hit the earth some 65 million years ago and killed all the dinosaurs. This did not happen, for two reasons. First, we know from the Bible that the earth is only 6,000 years old. Second, why would a meteor strike and kill the dinosaurs and leave the other animals alive? Yes, the dinosaurs did all die. After the Flood, and to this very day, there are many animals that have become extinct or are on the endangered species list because of the effects of sin on the earth. Animals become extinct for several reasons:

a. Because they are hunted.

b. Their land is destroyed.

c. They kill each other.

d. Their food supply runs out.

e. They get diseases that kill them.

That is probably exactly what happened to the dinosaurs. They all died.

How could Noah fit all the animals on the Ark?

First, the tremendous variety in species we see today did not exist in the days of Noah. Only the parent "kinds" of these species were required to be on board in order to repopulate the earth. For instance there were two dogs, not all the different types of dogs. There would have been approximately 1,500 kinds of animals on the ark which means approximately 7,000 animals and flying creatures.

How did Noah care for all the animals?

While Noah and his family took care and brought food enough, creation scientists suggest that God gave the animals the ability to hibernate, as we see in many species today. Most animals react to natural disasters in ways that were designed to help them survive.

How could a flood destroy every living thing? (Genesis 7:21-22).

Scripture tells us that the "fountains of the great deep" broke open. In other words, earthquakes, volcanoes, and geysers of molten lava and scalding water were squeezed out of the earth's crust in a violent, explosive upheaval. This did not stop until 150 days into the Flood—so the earth was literally churning underneath the waters for about five months!

This was much worse than the tsunami that killed 43,000 people or hurricane Katrina that we have experienced. "The world that then existed" was destroyed (2 Peter 3:3-6).

The earth separated from one land mass into 7 continents. The violent force of the flood changed everything.

Where did all the water go?

Simply put, the water from the flood is in the oceans and seas we see today. Three-quarters of the earth's surface is covered with water.

The average height of land is less than 5,000 feet. The ocean basins, on the other hand, are on the average 12,000 feet deep. If one were to somehow bulldoze the present land surface into the oceans so that the earth was absolutely level everywhere, at least a mile of water would cover everything. So that is where all the water is.

Was Noah's Flood global? (Genesis 7:19-20)

Some Christian's today claim that the flood of Noah's time was only a local flood. These people generally believe in a local flood because they have accepted the widely believed evolutionary history of the earth, which interprets fossil layers as the history of the sequential appearance of life over millions of years.

If Noah's flood had been local, God would have violated his Word many times over by the local floods that are happening all over the world.

First, the Bible tells us it was worldwide (Genesis 6-9 refers to "all flesh" 13 times). Genesis 7:19 states that the water rose above the highest mountains. Secondly, the biological evidence can be found in every continent today.

When people don't believe in the world wide flood, it's not because there is lack of evidence. The problem is that many scientists and people don't see it because they have accepted a different history of the earth.

Look at the evidence in the earth for Noah's Flood.

Evidence of Noah's Flood can be seen all over the earth, from sea beds to mountaintops.

In one year the pre-flood supercontinent was destroyed and a new world with seven continents rose from the waters. They are covered with layers of fossil-filled sediment deposited by water, testifying of the biblical account in Genesis.

The earth's crust has massive amounts of layered sedimentary rock, some areas miles deep. These layers of sand, soil, and material—mostly laid down by water—were once soft mud, but they are now hard stone. Encased in these sedimentary layers are billions of the dead (fossils of plants and animals) which were buried very quickly. The evidence all over the earth is staring everyone in the face.

A fossil is the remains, impressions, or trace of a living thing of a former geologic age, such as a skeleton or footprint, etc.

The earth before the flood.

The earth enjoyed a uniform sub-tropical climate everywhere. God created the earth for man. There were apparently no storms, wind, snow, ice, or floods. Water from springs prior to the flood was evidently abundant and a generous nightly mist or very heavy dew watered the ground.

Fossils of tropical plants can be found in Alaska today. Great coal beds have been discovered in Antarctica, and thousands of suddenly quick frozen warm-weather mammoth elephants were found in Siberia. The surface of the earth had been drastically altered as a result of the flood. The flood was a result of evil that filled the earth. The Grand Canyon and the Colorado River was evidence of a sudden catastrophic draining of a huge inland lake, etc. (Is Genesis History DVD 29:17-34:00)

Man was previously vegetarian, but after the flood was permitted to eat meat. Enmity entered the animal world. The animals began to fear man.

All of geology can be explained as the re-arranging of the earth's crust by the Flood. Consider the fact that it takes special conditions to make a fossil, and the world has billions of them in mass graves. Creatures must have been buried rapidly before they rotted or were eaten by scavengers. And, in fact, vast numbers of animals were buried and fossilized so quickly that some could not even finish swallowing their meal or give birth.

Another obvious evidence that makes sense of a global flood are fossils of tree trunks standing upright and others upside down through more than one layer. This doesn't make sense with the slow accumulation of layers over millions of years, but instead it is a sign of being buried rapidly. The Grand Canyon also contains multiple flat layers that are sitting on top of each other with no evidence of erosion in between. Also, you can go to many places on the planet and see row upon row of consecutively deposited rock layers that were soft when deposited and then bent, sometimes drastically. Rocks do not bend without breaking. They were bent before they could dry out and harden.

The evidence for the flood is everywhere, if your assumptions don't blind you from seeing it!

Why did people live so long before the flood?

Over the years people have speculated many reasons for the long age before the flood.

1. The earth had a thick water vapor canopy that blocked out most of the sun's harmful radiations.

2. The earth had a double atmospheric pressure that enhanced the health of all organic life.

3. Before the flood people ate much better and this extended their years on earth.

4. However, what seems to be the reason for such a long life seems to be found in genetics. Dr. David Menton and Dr. Georgia Purdom look specifically at genetics and resulting functions of anatomical features with regards to aging in their book "Did people like Adam and Noah really live over 900 years of age?" from the New Answers Book 2.

We need to keep in mind that there were two major genetic bottlenecks:

a. At the Flood

b. At the Tower of Babel

Genetic bottlenecks cause a significant loss of access to other people's versions of genes (called alleles) that are essentially lost. The obvious loss of pre-flood people reduced the alleles in the gene pool in humanity to only eight people, but really only six. So, this leaves Shem, Ham, and Japheth and their wives, and, of course, these three men each inherited their genes from the same two parents.

So, early generations after the flood, like early generations after the Garden of Eden, saw marriages between people who were close relatives. Of course, such close intermarriage was not forbidden until the time of Moses. Regardless, this bottleneck saw the loss of a great many alleles from the gene pool of those who died in the flood.

This happened again at the Tower of Babel as the people were dispersed and this reduced the gene pool again. The lifespan then dropped from 400's after the flood to 200's after the Tower.

So the Flood and the Tower bottlenecks did something significant to cause ages to drop. In both cases, there is a loss or splitting up of the gene pool.

Why do geology teachers believe the old earth theory?

I can't speak for all the teachers but after taking Geology 101 in college I know they believe in The Principle of Uniformitarianism, which means the present is the key to the past. Since geologic processes happen slowly today, they argue, the extensive rock and fossil records must have taken great lengths of time to form. However, the flood of the proportions described in Genesis would have resulted in vast amounts of erosion and re-depositing of sediments, fossilization of plants and animals, volcanism, and redistribution of radioisotopes. Like Charles Lyell, most of these scientists refuse to believe in the Bible or a worldwide flood. Consequently their picture of events in past history is limited to observations they make today. I personally sat down with a Christian geologist who does not believe in the story of Noah and the flood. Admittedly he has never read the Bible but doesn't believe this event ever happened, it was more of an allegory to him.

Kingdom Quiz (The World Wide Flood of Noah's Day)

1. After the flood of Noah's day how many people survived?
2. How long ago was this flood?
3. Were there more than 100,000 people who drowned in the flood?
4. What is geology?
5. How big was the Ark that Noah built?
6. When did the Ice Age take place?
7. How long ago did dinosaurs live?
8. How did Noah and his sons get all the animals in the Ark?
9. Was Noah's Flood regional or global?
10. Is there evidence to prove this flood?
11. What is Big Bone Lick?

THE ICE AGE AND ITS EFFECT ON THE EARTH

Glaciation during the Ice Age stretched across virtually all of Canada. The ice reached all the way to modern-day southern Illinois, and many of the northern states were covered. All of Antarctica as well as much of Europe and Russia were also covered. Therefore, Michigan would have been covered with glaciers.

The biblical view of the Ice Age gives evidence of only one taking place while the traditional view speaks of at least four different Ice Ages with advances and retreats.

When did the Ice Age take place? The Ice Age took place after Noah's Flood. The Genesis Flood actually caused the Ice Age. (DVD Is Genesis History 38:27-42:08) The Flood in Genesis 6, which occurred roughly 4,500 years ago, brought on one major Ice Age that lasted a few hundred years. After the flood, the climate of the earth was radically changed, and many forms of life which once existed became extinct.

The Bible gives us the big picture of human history. The order of biblical events is as follows:

1. Creation 2. Sin entered the world with a negative impact. 3. Noah's Flood, causing total worldwide destruction except for Noah, his family and the animals God brought to the ark. 4. The Ice Age 5. Recovery from the flood and the Ice Age. 6. Present day semi-stabilization. I say semi-stabilization because remnants of the Ice Age and glaciation are still present and changing.

The Ice Age probably began in the Northern Hemisphere and roughly coincides with the Babel judgment, (Genesis 11) around a century or so after the Flood. The two ingredients required for an Ice Age, cool temperatures and tons of snow, were dramatically fulfilled immediately after the Genesis flood. Based on the tremendous increase in precipitation rate and frequency of storms following the flood, glaciers thousands of feet thick would have developed over a few hundred years.

As a massive ice sheet expanded over Canada, it drove out most living things, and then it continued to push south into the Ohio valley. Eventually, the heavy snows stopped and the earth began warming again. (DVD-Is Genesis History-Bonus features 0-6:08)

The post-Flood climate was very different, with the collapse of the vapor canopy. The flood was so massive that the very crust of the earth broke apart (Genesis 7:11-12). The global flood brought unimaginable devastation and alteration to the earth that God created. The Ice Age followed this devastation. Earth's original continent broke up and spread apart. The dinosaurs, once contemporaries of men, rapidly died out.

Two particular aspects of the Flood were instrumental in causing the Ice Age:

1. Extensive volcanic activity during and after the Flood.

2. The warm oceans following the Flood. We know the extent of the Ice Age because the glaciers left features on the landscape similar to features we observe around glaciers today. The earth is still stabilizing and glaciers are still melting.

The flood event was so extensive the magma from the core of the earth was seeping up through cracks heating up the oceans. Oard and Vardiman (Vardiman, L., 1993, *Ice Cores and the Age of the Earth*, Technical Monograph, Institute for Creation Research, El Cajon, California) point to evidence that the ocean waters were in fact warmer just before the Ice Age, as recorded by the oxygen isotopes in the shells of tiny marine animas called foraminifera. This warm water caused extensive water vapors to be pulled up into the atmosphere. These processes that took place heated up the ocean temperatures to over 100 degrees Fahrenheit. This warm ocean set in motion a series of events that would cause the Ice Age. This would cause "super storms" dumping unheard of amounts of snow and ice in a short amount of time.

Then volcanic dust and debris were lofted into the atmosphere and stratosphere blocking the solar radiation from coming in which cooled the continents, especially the northern areas, in the lower elevations closer to equator this meant heavy rain.

Ice sheets and glaciers were formed in less than 500 years. There was a tremendous dynamic taking place for the first 1,000 years after the flood.

The vapor dropped tons upon tons of snow, causing ice to form, ice as much as a mile thick.

Meteorologist Michael Oard (*Ice Cores and the Age of the Earth* 1994) estimated that it would take about 700 years to cool the oceans down to what it is today.

We find a small example of this in Jack Williams research and writings, The epic volcano eruption that led to the 'Year Without Summer,' "The Washington Post, April 24, 2015. His research found Mt. Tambora blasted in 1815 and caused summer to cease in the Northern Hemisphere in 1816. It was estimated to drop the global temperature by 3 degrees Celsius. This was just one volcano! Volcanoes that send particles and dioxides into the upper atmosphere can cause severe weather problems—specifically causing summers to be cooler.

Just down the road from Cincinnati in the north central USA is Big Bone Lick, in Kentucky "the cradle of American paleontology." The discovery of huge bones from mastodons, giant sloths, and other Ice Age creatures sparked the first scientific expedition to collect vertebrate fossils in North America. In 1803, President Thomas Jefferson sent General William Clark to gather bones to ship to the White House. We recently visited this area where you can still find the white salt springs to which these animals were drawn.

After two centuries of research, there is enough information to begin recreating scenes from the rise and fall of the Ice Age. As a massive ice sheet expanded over Canada, it drove out most living things, and then it continued to push south into the Ohio valley. Eventually, the heavy snows stopped and the earth warmed. Once the ice began to melt, animals returned to Big Bone Lick. During the Ice Age, the thick ice sheets drew so much water out of the ocean that large tracts of ocean floor became dry ground. Herds of animals wandered across a 1,000 mile wide grassy plain that stretched from Asia across the Bering Strait to North America.

The effects of the Ice Age are still with us, particularly the giant ice sheets of Antarctica and Greenland, the alpine glaciers, and the glacial landforms and sediments. Because these effects are seen on the current land surface, it is clear that the Ice Age occurred after the Flood.

The ice never covered more than a third of the Earth's land surface, even at its greatest extent. At the same time as there was glaciation in the upper latitudes, there was probably a period of higher rainfall in the lower latitudes. Such higher rainfall towards the equator would have assured an abundant water supply even in present-day desert areas such as the Sahara, and Arabia. Archaeological excavations have yielded abundant evidence of lush vegetation, human occupation and complex irrigation economies in these now desolate regions.

There is also evidence that human societies lived near the edge of the ice sheet in Western Europe throughout the Ice Age—the Neanderthal people. Neanderthals were a group of humans, descended from Adam and Eve, who lived in the harsh post-flood world. Archaeology confirms they made instruments, make-up, jewelry, weapons, and ritually buried their dead. Many humans today share DNA with Neanderthals. This fully human lineage died out sometime after or during the Ice Age. A new genetic study, published in the journal, Science, compared the Neanderthal genome to the genes of five humans alive today. The comparison revealed that in some individuals, up to 4% of the total genome was of Neanderthal origin. Neanderthals were not only fully human but evidently were very skilled people coping with the harsh world of the post-flood Ice Age. They specialized in hunting the large, grazing animals that were abundant toward the end of the Ice Age. The word Neanderthal means primitive or unenlightened or barbaric or culturally or intellectually backward. Anthropologists now recognize that their somewhat brutish appearance was at least partly due to diseases (rickets, arthritis) caused by the dark, cold and damp climate of the region at that time. Their resulting lack of exposure to sunlight, which stimulates vitamin D synthesis necessary for normal bone development, and poor diet, would cause such rickets. They had physical features that helped them survive cold climates, like larger noses to humidify and warm dry, cold air and short, stout bodies to conserve heat. These people were not what some would call cave men or in the process of evolution. Their bodies had adapted to the cold weather, similar to the finches on the Galapagos Island. The same finches Darwin thought were evolving were in fact adapting to their environment. Aside from certain skeletal characteristics, Neanderthals were probably no different from other humans. These people simply lived in areas where their totally formed human bodies lacked the vitamins and minerals necessary for bones to grow properly and adapted to the cold environment. They were not primitive people as many have thought over the years. They were not the missing link between monkey and man many evolutionists wanted to claim. There is no reason why Neanderthals could not have lived at the same time as the advanced civilizations of Egypt, Babylon, and others that were developing unhindered in the lower latitudes. Neanderthals simply represent a people group that formed after the dispersion at the Tower of Babel, after the Flood, just a few thousand years ago. They had unique characteristics that likely became more prominent as they were isolated from other people by the divinely created language barrier.

Gene study tells us Native Americans came from Siberia over a land bridge from Siberia to North America (a land bridge since submerged in the Bering Straits). From there, the group populated the continent and diversified both genetically and culturally.

Woolly mammoths probably died after the Flood because there are thousands of carcasses scattered across Alaska and Siberia resting above flood deposits. There must have been sufficient time for the mammoths to have repopulated these regions after the flood. The post-flood Ice Age provides an explanation for the mystery of the wooly mammoths. Even in the northern regions where glaciation was present, close to the ocean was vegetation and growth because of the warm oceans. Thousands of these woolly mammoths became trapped in these regions with the increase of glaciers and therefore quickly died.

Accelerated melting would mark the end of the Ice Age.

Many pieces of the "Ice Age puzzle" remain unsolved, but one thing is sure. Based on the Bible, we can be certain that the changes occurred within a few human generations—not over millions of years.

As Christians, we must believe God's Word no matter what others believe and want us to believe! There is no empirical evidence to support neither four Ice Ages nor millions of year theories.

Let me ask you a question that is wrestled with in our world today! Is climate change natural or is it man caused by burning fossil fuels?

No one denies that climates have changed. But is man responsible for causing these changes? That question seems to be a political question, but it need not be. Let me explain. Is the average worldwide temperature even rising? Numerous factors contribute to global weather patterns—sunspot activity, greenhouse gases, volcanism—and experts can be found on either side of the climate debate. Man-made greenhouse gas emissions were certainly not responsible for two major periods of climate change centuries ago. The Medieval Warm Period (c. AD 800-1200) saw warmer than average temperatures that were even higher than the warmest years of the past few decades. The Little Ice Age (c. AD 1400-1880) brought cooler average temperatures than those experienced in modern times. Before the mid-1800's, there was little change in the amount of atmospheric carbon dioxide, so what caused these fluctuations? It certainly wasn't man burning fossil fuels. Many would point to the glaciers around the world melting away as evidence! The fact is they have been melting away for over 4,000 years. There has been global warming since the Ice Age that was generated by the flood of Noah. At one time glaciers covered one-third of the earth's surface!

This diagram shows those previous weather anomalies:

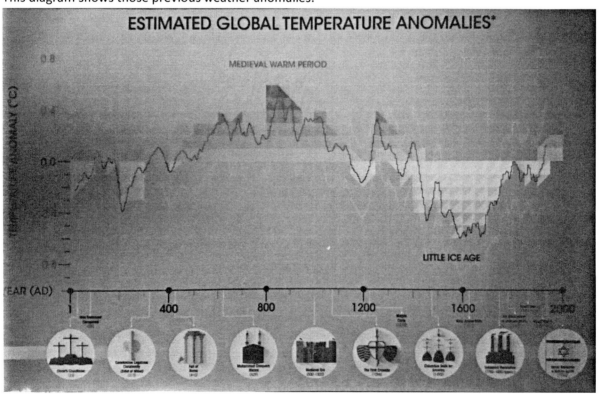

We have found remains of many land animals that have traveled to other continents. How is that possible? After the Flood, massive volumes of water would have remained on the land masses in inland seas. These long since have drained or dried up. A tremendous amount of water was trapped in the buildup of snow and ice on land. With so much water removed from the ocean, sea levels would have been hundreds of feet lower, exposing land bridges to nearly every continent on the globe.

So, if we reject or ignore the global flood and its ensuing Ice Age, all earth and geological sciences are flawed from their origin. Therefore, if fossils are dated using the rock layers where they are found, all the sciences is affected negatively by their flawed assumptions.

Kingdom Quiz (The Ice Age and Its Effect on the Earth)

1. When did the Ice Age take place?

2. How long did it last?

3. What are the two ingredients required for an Ice Age?

4. How thick were some of the glaciers?

5. What happened to the continents after the Flood?

6. Did Dinosaurs live 60 million years ago?

7. What warmed the oceans?

8. How long did it take to cool the oceans to what they are today?

9. What happened at "Big Bone Lick"?

10. Who sent General William Clark to get bones from "Big Bone Lick" and ship them to the White House?

If God is so Good, Why all the Suffering?

One of the greatest challenges in Christianity has to do with tragedies and unfair life circumstances. Why does a six month old baby die, or why is a child born with a life altering disease? Why does a mother die before raising her children? Even now as I prepare this message I have been contacted by family members to officiate at the funeral for one of our members. He was simply walking home from the store when an unidentified person shot and killed him, for no apparent reason. The list is endless of seemingly unfair and unanswerable questions.

This question has probably created more atheists than any other. While the answer is not simple, there are some indicators in God's Word that talk about some of life's circumstances.

Our answer to this question will tell us much about our ability to trust God. Many have resisted making a commitment to the Lord, because of their views on this subject.

Let me tell you up front, no one knows for sure why a Christian or non-Christian has to go through pain and suffering. Humanity has such limited knowledge that the only thing we really know is that our deepest parts scream that it's not right or fair.

Perspective can help us as we wrestle with this question. Perspective means a "point of view after viewing things or events in their true relationship to one another." **<u>Perspective means "seeing the panoramic view of things and how all the smaller scenes create one large panorama</u>**." If life was a simple 60-80 years on this earth, then the question would not make sense. But when we view life as God tells us, this earthly walk is simply part of an eternal journey. Our life is a comparatively short transitional period leading to eternity, and our time here is a training period. A time where the quality of our character is displayed and assessed by the amount of compassion we show to others; so that we are judged fairly on Judgment Day. The quality of compassion in a person's character is more evident when those around him or her are suffering.

The perspective of only seeing things with a physical earthly view puts great limitations on a person's understanding of God (Romans 8:18).

God sees the beginning from the end; He knows the whole picture. The worst physical circumstances of suffering may lead to physical death. But when a Christian becomes ill and God does not heal him or her on earth, the only other alternative is that their body dies and they go to Heaven. Christians always get healed, either here on earth or in a far better place (I Corinthians 15:55). Without truly believing, this life would definitely seem unfair.

Most Christians cannot answer the question about pain and feel helpless to defend the goodness of God when questioned about it, (as if God needs us to defend Him).

As believers, we hold these two truths about God dearly, but they seem to add to the dilemma:

1. *God is good.*
2. *God is all powerful and able to do anything.*

If these are true, (and we know they are), then why the unfair happenings? Why doesn't God eliminate all the pain and suffering?

Part of the dilemma is somewhat easier to accept than other areas. We know as long as people continue to do bad or evil things, other people will be hurt. If a drunk driver hits your car on your way home, you and possibly your family will suffer. As long as people make mistakes, there will be suffering.

We aren't supposed to like suffering. We weren't created to suffer. We were created to have joy. Yet, we do suffer, from our first heartbeat to our last. This is the effect of our broken, sinful world. It is part of being alive. But why?

Decent people often suffer, and those who do terrible evils often prosper. Jesus told us the rain falls on the just and the unjust alike (Matthew 5:45). This question of seemingly unfairness has been the subject of much discussion throughout history and is frequently spoken of in the Bible.

The "problem of pain," as C.S. Lewis once titled it, is atheism's most potent weapon against the Christian faith. They make one of two claims about God.

1. Either He is not a God of love and is indifferent to human suffering.
    or
2. He is not a God of power and, therefore is helpless to do anything about it.

Suffering is not a problem for all religions. However, it is for Christianity because we believe God is loving and good, and all powerful.

As God's creation we do not establish the standards of what is right. Only the Creator of all can do that (Romans 9:20).

We need to settle it in our minds and hearts, (whether we understand it or not), that whatever God does is, by definition, right and in our best interest (Genesis 18:25).

There is really no such thing as the "innocent suffering". In Romans 3:23, this scripture shows us that we are all guilty. Even infants, by nature, are born with the propensity to sin.

This entire world is under a great curse, (Genesis 3:17, Romans 8:21-22), and will continue to be until we occupy a new Heaven and a new Earth.

Why doesn't God just eliminate pain and evil?

Understanding why God allows evil and its' resultant suffering requires a fundamental understanding of one of God's greatest gifts; free will.

BIBLICAL REASONS FOR ALL THE PAIN

1. **The gift of a free will, or freedom of choice**. This freedom is necessary to establish righteous character (Deuteronomy 30:15-19). For free choice to operate, it is obvious that evil has to have the possibility of existing. Choosing to obey God and learning to love others when we have the freedom to do otherwise is vital for the future God has planned for us. Of all of God's creation, only man has the capacity for advanced decision making.

God gives us the ability to choose right or wrong. He encourages us to choose right (Deuteronomy 28:2). There are blessings for choosing right and curses for choosing wrong.

God has often tried to impress on man the crucial principle that every effect has a cause. But we have difficulty grasping this truth, so we continue to suffer the debilitating effects of our transgressions.

Sir Isaac Newton brought us the law of relativity, which states when an object is in motion "Every action has an opposite and equal reaction". We can believe this, but, find it hard to accept when our bad actions in life bring about bad results.

Actions yield consequences (Galatians 6:6-7, Proverbs 22:8). Part of the disbelief of this spiritual law may be that the result of the action may not be immediate. God often gives us time to recognize our error and ask for forgiveness, then turn from it. God calls this repentance.

Decisions have consequences. Many times suffering is simply the inevitable consequence of personal decisions. For example, often poverty can be traced to individual decisions. Students drop out of school, derailing their education and end up with a life of difficulty finding jobs, low wages and low self-esteem. Many teen girls become sexually active giving birth at young ages with no father in the picture. These children born out of wedlock are much more likely to use drugs, get in trouble, or drop out of school.

Many lives are cut short because of health issues. Poor eating habits with little exercise affect our health and wellbeing.

2. **This world is not the way God created it, but is the result of sin, disease, sickness and crime**. There was a time on this earth when suffering and sorrow did not exist. When God first created man upon the earth, everything was perfect. It was God's plan for man to live in peace and harmony; never having to experience sorrow. After Adam sinned everything changed (Genesis 3). The laws of nature treat everyone the same. If you come in contact with a person with a contagious disease, you run the risk of catching it. The laws of nature do not make exceptions for nice people. Bonnie and I recently visited our daughter in Florida and while working in her yard I picked up a good amount of poison ivy and ended up in the clinic. This planet is not a safe place.

3. **Sometimes people suffer for the salvation of the lost**. Watching others go through tragedies can actually bring some people to Christ. When Lazarus was sick Jesus knew it, but did not come to him until he was dead. The Bible tells us it was because of his death that many came to Christ (John 12:11). William Tyndale was burned at the stake in 1520.

His crime was that he translated the Bible from Hebrew and Greek to English, the language of the people of England. He suffered and died so millions could read the Word of God.

This can only be understood when we view life the way God wants us to. For most people a "good life" means that they make a comfortable living, enjoy good health, and then die peacefully at age 80. To some extent, this is true. But, we have a soul and there is such a thing as eternity, so the picture changes entirely. Eighty years in the face of eternity is not such a big deal. The Bible tells us we now see life through a glass darkly. God sees eternity. This simply means we can't always understand why life turns out the way it does and that is why we need to trust the One who has the panoramic view of our lives. We only see the close up shots. God plans life a little farther out than we do! He sees farther than 80 years ahead. He has always existed and will always be.

The movie _"Soul Surfer"_ is a true story about Bethany Hamilton, a Christian who had her arm bitten off by a shark. As she cried out to God for the answer why, God showed her how thousands of people heard of her determination and wanted to go on with life because she did.

4. **Sometimes the suffering and pain of unsaved men is used by the Holy Spirit to cause them to realize their need for salvation.** Suffering can make people want to search for God. From a Christian perspective, if that's what inspires them to follow Him, and they end up in heaven because of it, then ultimately, it works out for the good. When Israel forgot God, and began serving other gods, God actually became their enemy (Judges 2:11-15).

5. **The pain and suffering that Christians go through should also be the means of developing a stronger dependence on God and a more Christ-like character** (Hebrews 12:5-11). It can actually make our lives more fruitful. What we perceive as punishment can actually be an opportunity for growth. We learn more about God during these crisis moments than any other time in our lives. As the psalmist tells us, "Yea though I walk through the shadow of death the Lord is with me". We grow when we have to extend ourselves. During dry seasons plants grow their roots deeper to reach water and nutrients that makes them much stronger and resistant to adversity.

6. **God may allow suffering in our lives as a test of our obedience and faithfulness.** God often has plans for our lives but cannot use us until we have proven ourselves to be faithful and trustworthy. Before we can be used for His glory, we need to be faithful. Before God called Abraham the father of the faith, he had to prove he was trustworthy. He had to offer his only son on the altar in obedience to God. God did not want Abraham to kill his son; He just wanted to see if he would do it (Genesis 22:1-2). Joseph had to go through years of adversity, being thrown into a pit, falsely accused of a crime, and put into jail before God could trust him to be a part of saving the known world from a great famine (Genesis 37-50). Jonah had to spend three days in the belly of a whale before God could use him to save an entire city. Jesus had to suffer and die to save the entire world.

7. **Seeing people less fortunate and suffering can cause people to dedicate their lives to helping others, or to simply change their attitudes.** After pioneering Old Town, Bonnie and I saw many people who were suffering financially and going without adequate food and clothing. This led us to begin a simple mobile soup kitchen. It has expanded greatly and now serves hundreds of people every week.

8. **The Bible tells us that God can actually cause painful events to happen in our lives in order to purify us**. Heat can be a purifying agent, it brings impure elements to the surface to be dealt with and removed. This is also called pruning (John15:2).

9. **Much of the suffering in the world would be eliminated if humanity followed Biblical instructions**. Suffering caused by greed/profiteering, domestic violence, unwanted pre-marital pregnancy, incest, murder, and excessive alcohol use would be eliminated if we followed God's instructions. This would also include the suffering caused by sexually transmitted diseases and many of the other diseases that have plagued humanity.

10. **It may be that in God's foreknowledge, He knows that if a person is left on the earth they would suffer more pain, hurt and sorrow.** Isaiah 57:1NLT "Good people pass away; the godly often die before their time. But no one seems to care or wonder why. No one seems to understand that God is protecting them from the evil to come". Or God may know the person can't handle future problems, temptations and trials and will take them out to spare them. Upon death, children go straight to Heaven. Until they reach the point of understanding God's presence, and reject Him by doing their own thing. Their salvation is secure. Even though God gives us free will to choose or reject Him, He can see into our future and knows who on this earth will accept Him. He also knows that some people will face a life of pain, suffering and trials through choices made for them or by them. God may rescue some children to heaven before their hearts harden against Him under the influence of the world. For others, perhaps, He rescues from a life of pain and trauma which is in their future but which they cannot possibly see.

11. **Suffering can cause joy to be more intensified.** Someone who has had a scare with death may think of life as more precious and therefore take more delight in it than someone who has always taken it for granted. The fictitious story of Scrooge gives us a picture of this principle. He was a stingy, mean, old rich man until introduced to his mortality causing him to change his life. While this particular story may not be true, the principle has happened to countless people who have experienced a life altering event.

12. **Another reason God allows suffering is so that we can demonstrate His loving compassion by meeting the needs of others.** Mother Theresa is a good example of a person seeing the suffering in Calcutta, India then dedicating her life to help those in need. If people did not have needs, then there would be no demonstrations of compassion. If one of the characteristics God wants us to develop and possess for His future Kingdom is compassion, then we need to have opportunities to show and develop it.

13. **Sometimes God allows us to endure trials, tribulations, and sufferings so that we can empathize with others going through the same thing (2 Corinthians 1:3-5NIV).** If Christians never faced pain and sorrow, we would not be able to help others going through difficulties because we couldn't relate to them. In the movie _"Courageous"_, the key actor lost his 9 year old daughter when a drunk driver killed her. After he went through the grieving process, he became a better father and was able to help many other men become better fathers (the movie Courageous 1:56:23-2:01:27).

14. **There are times when God brings situations into our lives that cause us to seek Him. This is so that we can receive the blessings of seeking Him (2 Chronicles 7:13-14).** He allows or causes circumstances in our lives to draw us back when we pull away from Him (Psalms 78:34-35). When God brings tribulation upon a people, they lose their pride, pray, and seek the face of God. They turn away from everything else and look to the Lord. I believe our nation is at the brink of a great awakening/revival because of the calamity this country and world is about to experience.

15. **Some believers go through trials for the purpose of refining them** (Daniel 11:35 NKJV). Each of us consumes large quantities of gasoline as fuel, and oil products every year. We do not realize the many products that are derived from the raw oil that is taken from the ground, including crayons, plastics, heating oil, jet fuel, kerosene and the tires on our automobiles. When is the last time you thought about how that oil becomes gas or kerosene? This oil is sent to refineries where it is pumped into holding tanks waiting to be refined. In the refining process the hydrocarbon molecules in the oil are separated into compounds by using various boiling points. They are then separated by distillation into the desired element. This refining process uses heat and time which alters the original product to become the desired end result. This is similar to the refining process God uses, heat and time should bring the desired result if the original element responds well to the refining.

16. **God wants us to be totally dependent upon Him, and suffering seems to bring us to that point** (2 Corinthians 4:16-17). The Bible presents us with a paradox. A paradox is a statement or belief that seems to contradict common belief. Parents raise children to become independent and able to live on their own someday. So we become independent adults capable of taking care of ourselves. After becoming a Christian God wants us to trust in Him and come to Him with all of our concerns, needs, cares and problems. Proverbs 3:5-6 tells us to "Trust in the Lord with all your heart, and lean not on your own understanding; in all your ways acknowledge Him, and He shall direct your paths". We must learn to live independently yet be dependent upon God for all our needs. Life has to be reshuffled and relearned and the process can be difficult. Sometimes God has to bring us to the end of our independence to realize we aren't as in control as we think we are. This journey can mean trials and pain as we learn to rely upon the Lord.

17. **God will also use suffering to teach us patience.** Romans 5:3 tells us that "tribulation worketh patience". Patience is the ability to wait or endure without complaint; it is steadiness, endurance, or perseverance. Unfortunately, the only way to grow in patience is to be placed in situations where you need patience.
18. **Some suffering in the life of a Christian can be the result of sin or losing focus in life**. In Numbers 21:6-9, God sent fiery serpents among the Israelites, causing them to admit that they had sinned. When the people turned to God in repentance, He instructed Moses to craft a bronze serpent and place it on a pole and those who were doomed to die could look at the bronze serpent and live. Suffering can take on many forms. All suffering is not from God, but He does have means to get our undivided attention.

As you can see, from the list of possibilities there are many reasons why pain in life happens.

Sometimes, however, it's best not to look for explanations for suffering. They won't necessarily be found easily. The Bible says in Deuteronomy 29:29 "The secret things belong to God". There are many times in life we will not have answers but will just need to trust God and go on with life. Sometimes, any positive effects may not become apparent until years later.

I have seen much suffering over the years, and it seems to me that the key is "attitude". How people deal with it depends upon their attitude. Some people are angry or hurt to such an extent that they never go beyond a particular event. The result then becomes the defining moment of their lives.

For some, an unfair or terrible life crisis seems to be their ticket to dismiss God and never revisit Him or church again. While they may never find the reason for the unfair event, surely running from God will cause untold devastation in their lives and into eternity. Often, over time, these people build walls of separation between them and God. Through the years the walls are reinforced and their hearts become so hard it would take a jack hammer to open them up to God. The Holy Spirit convicts and draws us to Christ, but our will is still involved.

When Christians see their suffering from the point of view of eternity, it can seem less significant (Romans 8:16-18).

What about Healing and Deliverance?

As Bible believing Christians we believe that God still heals and delivers people today. When believers go through difficult times and aren't delivered and don't seem to have that "abundant life", they sometimes question their faith or God. One of the greatest principles presented in the Bible is the story of three Hebrew young men; Shadrach, Meshach, and Abednego. Daniel chapter three has the full story. They were living in a foreign land ruled by a pagan king. These three young men were ordered to bow down and worship an image of King Nebuchadnezzar and if they refused they would be thrown into a large fiery furnace. Because they worshiped and served the One true God Shadrach, Meshach and Abednego would never bow down to an image of another god. Their response to the king was, "Our God whom we serve is able to deliver us from the burning fiery furnace, and He will deliver us from your hand, O king. But if not, let it be known to you, O king, that we do not serve your gods, nor will we worship the gold image which you have set up" (Daniel 3:17-18). These men had not only faith in God, but also in His deliverance. Whether or not God delivered them the young men still trusted and would serve Him even if it meant their lives. God did rescue them from the furnace. But, in another book of the Bible we find a much different ending. Hebrews chapter eleven give us a list of men and women who were rescued and delivered from trials. However, the end of that same chapter lists many that were not rescued, but underwent great trials and some dying for their faith.

These were not "lesser" saints because they found no miracle. If anything they were "greater" because they were faithful, even when things didn't work out the way they'd hoped for.

God tells us in His Word, "When you pass through the waters, I will be with you; and when you pass through the rivers, they will not sweep over you. When you walk through the fire, you will not be burned; the flames will not set you ablaze" (Isaiah 43:2).

Years ago many Christians read of a new and immediately popular book called "The Prayer of Jabez". In this book they were challenged to pray a prayer found in I Chronicles 4:10. In this prayer Jabez asked God, "Oh that You would bless me indeed, and enlarge my territory, that Your hand would be with me, and that You would keep me from evil, that I may not cause pain". In his commentary the author states when we pray this prayer the result is prosperity, miracles, and financial blessings. Believers grabbed this new teaching and begin to pray for prosperity and enlargement; this became their focus. I believe this type of teaching can create unstable Christians, who only want prosperity and can't handle anything other than that. Life throws us many curves; no matter what the result we need to run, not walk, to God for help, comfort, peace and hope. Like those three Hebrew men, I know my God is able to rescue me. But even if He doesn't, I will not try to second guess Him. I will continue to serve Him and trust Him.

 To understand this whole issue of pain and suffering for a Christian, as your pastor, I want to help clear up a misconception about the way the Gospel is often presented.

The primary purpose of Christ's sacrifice always was, and always will be, that believers will escape the upcoming Judgment and wrath of God. However, what is frequently preached is that God has a wonderful plan for your life, wants to solve your problems, make you happy in Christ, and rescue you from the hassles of this life.

When people are drawn to Christ with this offer, they will soon walk away. You may have noticed I do not give a conventional "altar call". The altar call was not used by the early church. In fact it was first used by Evangelist Charles Finney in 1820. Other same era evangelists like George Whitefield, Jonathan Edwards, and John Wesley had never even heard of an altar call. For Finney the "walking forward" became a public profession of one's faith. However, this caused great doctrinal confusion because the Biblical profession of faith was and still is, water baptism.

I don't call people forward at the end of the service because there is a great danger if people are not ready to come forward, and totally commit to Christ. One must know what they are committing to before they make the decision to forsake the world and follow Christ. It is my responsibility to preach the Word. There should be a call to make a decision that comes in the message and then we allow the Holy Spirit to act upon, convict and draw people to Christ. If a person's emotions are manipulated to produce a decision, and if they truly don't know what they're doing, then it's not conversion, and will not last. When a person hears God has a wonderful plan for their life, they are thinking of things like happiness, prosperity, health, joy and peace. Then when problems come and they are not happy with the way life seems to be working out, they may feel cheated and lied to then end up walking away from their commitment to the wonderful life.

This is why so many walk away from Christ and the rate of retention is so low at large crusades. God never promised us a problem or trouble free life. But He does promise to walk with us through the valleys (Psalms 23).

Imagine two men being handed parachutes as they board an airplane. One man was told the parachute would make his flight more comfortable and would take care of all the bumps along the way. The second man was told the plane might go down and the chute would save him from the crash.

About midway in the flight, the first man realized the chute didn't make his flight more comfortable and he still felt all the bumps. Besides that, the other passengers were laughing at him so he took his chute off for the remainder of the flight. The second man was just as uncomfortable, but didn't mind the people laughing at him because he had been told the plane might go down and he would be safe.

At the time of conversion, we must not tell half-truths. New believers must learn to hold on to God through tough times as well as peaceful times.

The Bible does say God has a plan for our lives. Jeremiah 29:11 says "I know the thoughts that I think towards you, says the Lord, thoughts of peace and not of evil, to give you a future and a hope". God does have plans for us in the future, in this life and in eternity. This does not mean life won't be difficult and hurt at times. I don't want anyone making a commitment to Christ thinking that now life will be trouble free with no hidden hurts and pains. Try to tell the story of the good life to the Apostle Paul, or Peter who died for their faith. Tell it to those in Foxes Book of Martyrs or to the Christians who were thrown to the lions in the coliseum, or to the 171,000 who are martyred for their faith every year. Tell William Tyndale God had a wonderful plan for his life as he was being burned to death. Does God still have a future and hope for them? They have arrived and are basking in that future and hope now. For each of us, it may be awhile yet.

Can you see me calling people to Christ at the end of the service and telling them God has a wonderful plan for their lives? He wants to give them happiness and fill that God shaped hole in their lives. He wants to give them abundant life and heal their bodies. Then as they are coming forward, they see us praying for those in our church who are going through cancer treatment or are preparing for surgery. Or they notice us praying for another who just lost their job or for someone whose child was diagnosed with a life altering illness. What happened to the wonderful plan for them, or the trouble free life? Where is the abundant life promised?

In this life there will be tribulation, (John 15:20), but be of good cheer, we have a better life promised and when we go through trials we aren't alone.

When people come to the Lord for the wrong reason, not only will they not remain, but they are not true converts. The Bible tells us there is only one true plan of salvation and it has to do with repentance from sin and asking Jesus into our lives. We don't come to Christ for the good life but for eternal life.

The person in the Bible who suffered more than anyone was Job. He learned much through the loss of his children, wealth, health and prestige. Even at the end of his suffering, he never knew why it all happened but he did learn much about God. Job's knowledge of God caused him to have total faith in God, regardless of how bad his temporary suffering was. Job stated "Though He slay me, yet will I trust Him" (Job13:15).

Trust the One who is for you and guides you through the tragedies of life, even though you don't know why they come.

In Summary

1. Suffering is a necessary part of the Christian life. It is part of our experience as we travel from here to eternity. You may think you would only want pleasure without suffering; however you wouldn't truly enjoy it. I learned in the U.S. Marines, "No pain, no gain".
2. God uses our present suffering to prepare us for future glory (Romans 8:18-27). In the Marine Corps "Boot Camp", our basic training lasted four months. "Life" is the believer's basic training and it is preparation for eternity. God uses everything in our lives to prepare us for future glory. In the life to come, all the pain and suffering won't even be remembered.

Our suffering cannot separate us from the love of God. Romans 8:38-39 tells us "For I am persuaded that neither death nor life, nor angels nor principalities nor powers, nor things present nor things to come, nor height nor depth, nor any other created thing, shall be able to separate us from the love of God which is in Christ Jesus our Lord." He loves us as much in the valley as He does on the mountain top. Job's suffering took many things away from him, but not the love of God. No matter what you go through, God loves you and will never leave you. He is the one who comforts and strengthens us to be able to face life, no matter what it brings. Once we see His face, all this will be forgotten. But until then, our trust in Him is what will carry us through the dark time.

Kingdom Quiz (If God is all Good, Why all the Suffering?)

1. Is God all powerful?
2. Can God do anything?
3. God gave Adam and Eve along with you and me a _____ _____.
4. Is the world today the way God created it?
5. Who sets the standard of right and wrong?
6. Sir Isaac Newton brought us the law of relativity, "Every action has an opposite and equal _____.
7. Who are the 3 Hebrew young men who were thrown into the fire?
8. What was the great principle they taught us?

What is the Purpose of Life?

Life is short. So short, in fact, that the Bible says it is as a vapor that appears for a little while and then vanishes (James 4:14). Life is a journey. We are all traveling inevitable towards the end of our lives. Every one of us will either coast through life with no sense of direction or live with purpose and fulfilment. Purpose flows out of values. Every time we make a decision in life, we are filtering that decision through our values, whether we're conscious of it or not. We all have values and those values affect everything we do. Often we haven't clarified or examined them. This is also called your 'world view' or how you think the world works. Once becoming a Christian we are to now begin to re-think that world view and begin to transform our thinking (Romans 12:1-2). Reading the Bible we find that life on this Earth is a temporary assignment (Psalm 39:4-5). In the Marine Corps they call it temporary assigned duty, or TAD. I was stationed in California, Okinawa, Vietnam, and North Carolina. At the time it seemed as if it was eternity but looking back fifty years, I see how short that really was. In Eternity when we look back on this life we will realize its brevity. So live now knowing that it is short and do all you can for the glory of God during this brief time He gives us. God helps us in this life and even gives us the very breath we breathe and if He were to neglect us only for a few seconds we would cease to live. We are totally dependent on God for breath and life. As the Apostle Paul said, "In Him we live and move and have our being" (Acts 17:28).

Because life is so short we do not want to waste it on things that don't amount to a 'hill of beans'. But first life's great question must be answered; the one people have asked for centuries, "Is there any meaning to the time that I spend in this world?"

When we find the meaning of life, that meaning should help us answer the three questions many people have asked:

1. Does my life have real purpose: is it directing me toward some goal or end? Am I standing for something?
2. Does my life have significance: does it count for anything as part of a greater whole? What does my life contribute to the universe as a whole? What does it count for in the grand scheme of things?
3. Does my life have value? Is my life worth anything overall? Is the world a better place for having my life as part of it?

There is something about funerals that causes us to look back at life and how brief it seems to be. Because of Old Town's community exposure we officiate at many funerals. There are three basic purposes for a funeral or memorial service:

1. To comfort family and friends of the deceased.
2. To speak to the living about the brevity of life and the length of Eternity. Sharing the Gospel with the living and explaining their need for Christ.
3. To honor the deceased by reflecting on their past history on Earth along with passions they had during the brief time of their life.

I always encourage family and friends to honor their loved one by speaking about their desire for life which memorializes them. Sadly, I rarely hear anything that speaks of a person's legacy for their family or others. It grieves me to see a life come and go with nothing of value left behind. It makes me want to declare to the living what the true purpose of one's life should be. For instance, the only thing anyone could say about one man was that his lawn was the best in the neighborhood; another was his passion for hunting and fishing. Is that it?

Don't get me wrong, enjoying activities in life is fine but it just should not be a person's signature identity. I also work at keeping my lawn groomed well, but hopefully that won't be my legacy left behind. While the future is hopefully where every person's eternal rewards await them, we should be leaving a legacy that has helped others through the maze of this life.

We will all die one day, so what will be the true meaning of our brief time in this world? What will we be remembered by? Is there purpose to what we are doing? To what should we devote our earthly time and efforts? In the end, or a common phrase today "at the end of the day," what really matters? C.S. Lewis once said, "Human life has always been lived on the edge of a precipice."

Do we really know our purpose, or are we caught up in the rat race of our society allowing the world to pull us into the pursuit of the so—called good life?

Pascal, the French physicist and philosopher, wrote: "There is a God-shaped vacuum in the heart of every man which cannot be filled by any created thing, but only by God the Creator, made known through Jesus Christ."

Once a person fills that void with Christ, their quest should be to discover their purpose in life. This will be a process through building a friendship with God. Although the idea of being God's friend might seem far-fetched to some, the Bible gives us this encouragement, "Draw close to God, and He will draw close to you" (James 4:8; 2:23). Christianity is not a religion or a philosophy, but a relationship and a lifestyle.

The meaning of life is one of the most frequently asked questions by humanity since the beginning of time. It is questioned by people who have the ability to make choices about life; searching for truth and purpose along the way.

God has a purpose for everything He creates, including each of us (Isaiah 45:18). There is order, system and design to the whole of creation. Man is the highest expression of God's creation, created with the highest intelligence. None of us will be truly fulfilled until we invite Christ to show us the very purpose for which He created us.

When individuals do not know or understand the true meaning of our time here on Earth they will establish their own meaning to life, and most do. Some will seek after riches and wealth as their meaning to life. Others the need for power becomes their drive and purpose. For some it may be fame, beauty, sports, shopping, entertainment, education, or a great career. The purpose in life was answered by Albert Einstein when he said, "A life directed chiefly towards the fulfillment of personal desires will sooner or later always lead to bitter disappointment" (Letter to T. Lee, January 16, 1954).

Have you ever felt there must be something more; something beyond merely existing? A man was waiting for his golfing partners at a local golf course restaurant and said to the waitress, "there must be more to life than this." It didn't take long before she invited him to come to her church (Old Town) to learn more about the purpose of life. The same man later went to work and was talking with a fellow employee who was reading a Bible on his break and he asked this man the same question. The fellow worker told the man that he should come to his church to hear about this "more to life" subject; he told him his church was Old Town Christian Outreach Center. Again, later that week, while at the Saginaw YMCA, he was talking with another man in the sauna when he made the same declaration. This man told him he needed to come to his church to hear more on the subject. You guessed it; he was once again invited to Old Town Christian Outreach Center.

After three encounters in just one week he brought his wife to Old Town on Sunday where they both came to find their purpose in life, and are now followers of Christ.

There is something very deep within us shouting that there is more to life! God tells us there is something great and meaningful for our lives (Romans 1:16-20).

This does not mean we can't have fun and enjoy our life, it just means we must understand the important things and prioritize.

What is it that gives meaning to life? Are we left to find our own purpose, or is there ever any meaning to life at all? These are questions that need to be answered before we come to the end of our lives, answers that will bring honor, purpose and fulfillment. This life is preparation for Eternity. Knowing your purpose will help prepare you for that eternity.

Before tackling this frequently asked subject about our purpose in life we first must establish ones belief about the origin of life. For instance, if one believes they are simply part of an evolving species, then they have no purpose other than existence and survival of the fittest. The theory of biological evolution requires that nonliving chemicals somehow developed completely by chance into highly complex, living organisms. This theory fits more in the realm of science fiction than science. If this were true then meaning to life is what the individual decides it to be, or whatever is important to them. Evolution tells us there is no meaning to life and that there is also a connection between evolution and morality. The more a person or people believe that life arouse by natural processes, the more they will also believe that life is ultimately meaningless and without purpose and morality can be whatever a person determines. Then who is to say what is right and wrong? So everyone should be able to do what is right for them (Judges 21:25)?

The simple cell that Charles Darwin thought to be a blob of protoplasm ends up, we find, after the invention of the electron microscope, to contain one hundred thousand million atoms; far more complicated than man could ever imagine. Within that "simple cell", are thousands of small irreducibly complex motors in operation. Which is impossible to evolve one piece at a time even if there were millions of years. For an evolutionist this life is all there is. You are nothing special and life has no value because we are on an evolutionary journey to who knows where. By the way, the real shock will take place the instant a non-Christian takes their last breath. But God is so good He allows us to believe whatever we want even if it isn't to serve Him.

On the other hand, if someone believes they were created by God, then He must have created them for a purpose. An all-powerful, all knowing God would not create anything without a purpose.

Upon much investigation it becomes quite clear the theory of evolution cannot stand the test of truthfulness or science. Therefore, should quickly be eliminated by a thinker and researcher. This leaves only one other possibility; that an all-powerful and all-knowing God created mankind. The Bible tells us God has made us, "The Spirit of God has made me, and the breath of the Almighty gives me life" (Job 33:4).

The human body is designed unlike any other creature. Our ability to communicate and understand, to feel emotions, and think rationally shows that we are created for a purpose.

Sigmund Freud helped answer the question of life when he said, "Only religion can answer the question of the purpose of life. One can hardly be wrong in concluding that the idea of life having a purpose stands and falls with the religious system" (Civilization and its Discontents, 1930).

Our culture teaches us that the real purpose in life is simply to be happy. This belief brings confusion because no one is happy all the time. Finding a life of meaning, and purpose, is the secret to dealing with the stress, problems, and hopelessness that can plague our everyday lives. When you discover your ultimate purpose, the incidental problems in life pale when compared to the fulfillment your purpose brings.

The Bible is our source to discover our individual and specific purpose in life. In the Bible we find that God is calling us out of our everyday mundane life of self-centeredness into a dynamic life of purpose. It is about transformation into what we were designed to be (Luke 14:33; Revelation 21:7).

God loves you the way you are, but He does not want you to stay there. He wants you to discover your purpose while being transformed into the image of Christ. God has given us a pattern to follow, and that is to become imitators of Christ (Ephesians 5:1).

You have a very specific purpose in this world, but you also have a choice. You don't have to respond to God's purpose. You can just keep going on the way you have been and ignore God's calling for your life. Many believers come to know Christ but never find or fulfill their purpose in life. We are all stewards of God's creation and He has given us talents, desires and passions to be used to care for His possessions. We will give account to Him someday for the gifts He has given us and what we did with them.

Jesus teaches us in the Parable of the Talents (Matthew 25:14-30) that we must use the talents He has given us. The talent was first used as a measure of weight (about 75 pounds) and then as currency or money. **This parable warns us that our place and service in Heaven will depend on our faithfulness and service on Earth.** In this parable a talent represents our ability, time, resources and opportunity to serve God (and others) while on Earth. God has entrusted all of these things to us, and He expects us to use and apply these gifts in the wisest possible way so that Christ can see a return on His investment.

These talents aren't for us but to be used for others and for the Kingdom of God. This parable teaches us five things:

1. Success is a product of our work. We are to work, using our talents to glorify God. The word "work" is found over 500 times in the Bible.
2. God gives us everything we need to accomplish what He has called us to do. The servants were given enough to produce more and it is the same with the gifts God has given us.
3. The parable shows that our gifts are not equal. Each servant was given according to his ability. The master understood that the one-talent servant was not capable of producing as much as the five-talent servant. He measured success by degree of effort, not how much each was given.
4. This parable teaches us to work for the Master, not for our own selfish purposes. The money given to the servants was not their own. What they earned with the capital was not theirs to keep.
5. This parable tells us that we will be held accountable. It is not about salvation or works of righteousness, but about stewardship of the gifts and talents given to us by God. **What the followers of Christ receive in the future kingdom of God will depend on how much they lay hold of and pursue God's purposes now.**

Jesus gives us the general purpose for all Christians; love and serve God, and love and serve others (Matthew 22:37-39; Mark 12:29-31; Luke 10:25-27). The Bible also tells us that we each have a very specific purpose in life.

We have found here at Old Town that volunteering or giving of our time and resources to help those in need is one of the most powerful sources of meaning and purpose, and is also tremendously fulfilling (Philippians 2:4). All the ministries of this church function by volunteers fulfilling their God given purpose in life. The Lord revealed to me years ago my ministry was to help others find and fulfill their purpose in this life.

Real life is filled with fulfillment, acceptance and purpose. This can only take place when we find and fulfill our God given specific purpose. The Apostle Paul came to the end of his life and said he had completed the race set before him (2 Timothy 4:7-8). Finding and finishing the course set for each of us is every believers challenge.

When a believer discovers and fulfills his life's purpose and eventually leaves this life for Eternity their memorial service will truly be a celebration, with no regrets and they will leave behind a powerful legacy. But the real reward will be the one sent ahead of them in Heaven for Eternity.

This is our future when we die. Understanding this will help us to live a sacrificial life for Christ in this life. Knowing what happens immediately after death will also help those left behind, so they will not grieve like those who have no hope. Death for Christians is not the end of life but actually the beginning. All the troubles of this life are over (2 Corinthians 4:17). We will immediately receive a heavenly body (2 Corinthians 5:1-5). It means we will be with others who have died before us. We will meet family members we may have never known (Genesis 25:8). Physical death is a door into the very presence of God (Philippians 1:23). Physical death is entering into a peace like we have never known (Isaiah 57:1-2). The believer exists in full consciousness (Luke 16:19-31). Activities in Heaven will include worship, celebration and singing, assigned tasks (Luke 19:17) and eating and drinking (Luke 14:15; 22:14-18; Revelation 22:2). Believers in Heaven will continue to maintain their personal identity (Matthew 8:11; Luke 9:30-32). Some have become confused when reading I Thessalonians 4:13-18 about the resurrection of the dead when they receive their resurrected bodies. Before this resurrection and while waiting in Heaven we will not be invisible spirits without a body but will have a temporary heavenly form (Luke 9:30-32; 2 Corinthians 5:1-4).

The Bible declares human purpose in two ways. First, there is a general purposefulness about human life. Second, there is an individual purpose in life.

God has a specific purpose for every person. "For we are God's workmanship created in Christ Jesus to do good works, which is prepared in advance for us to do" (Ephesians 2:10).

There are eight purposes in life for all of mankind. The first seven are the general purposes for everyone but the eighth is the unique individual purpose.

Your purpose in life is:

1. You were created to know God. Not just know Him intellectually but personally as well. Adam was created by God to have this type of close personal relationship with Him. God would walk and talk with Adam in the cool of the day. However, sin broke that close relationship. Now, because our sins have been atoned for, we again can have that close relationship if we pursue it. This only comes from a close relationship with Him; not in a religious way but in a personal way. This is where much of the organized church today does not understand. Organized religion has formalized as well as ritualized away any idea of having a personal relationship with God. A relationship that can only be developed through intimate time with Him while reading the Bible, His love letter and His self-revelation for us. Without relationship building we can only learn what others tell us about Him.

To truly know God is to have a personal, first hand relationship with Him. The enemy of your soul does not want you to know and believe in God, so he does everything he can to keep you from this truth (I Peter 5:8; 2 Corinthians 4:3-4). Your enemy does not want you to find your purpose in life but wants to keep you seeking only pleasures and earthly desires.

2. You were created for God's glory (Isaiah 43:6-7). According to the Bible, our purpose and reason we are here, is for God's glory. He created humanity to display His glory, so that His glory might be known and praised. God created us for this: to live our lives in a way that makes Him look more like the greatness and the beauty and the infinite worth that He really is. When we glorify God, we are reflecting how awesome and amazing He is through our actions and attitudes. We are meant to display to the world what He is really like. His glory can be shown in many practical ways. His glory shines at Old Town every time we feed the hungry and offer clothes to needy people. When we minister in the jail, to pregnant women, to those struggling with addictions, or lonely seniors His glory radiates (Matthew 5:16). When they, and our community, see these good works they will glorify our Father in Heaven.

   Every good work should be a revelation of the glory of God. This displays His glory to the angelic hosts and to all of His creation. We are not the only ones that display God's glory, "The Heavens declare the glory of God, and the sky above proclaims His handiwork" (Psalm 19:1). Our salvation is for God's sake. We were created to show His greatness and splendor to a world that does not know Him. In I Chronicles 16:28-29 we are told to ascribe glory to our God by praise and worship and by bringing an offering to Him. That offering is our obedience and submission to what He commands us; in other words obedience (I Samuel 15:22). The Westminster Shorter Catechism states, "Man's chief end is to glorify God, and to enjoy Him forever." Glorifying God is the end result of the Christian life. While we cannot add to God's glory, we can reflect and magnify, His glory in our lives, and this is what we are called to do. This should naturally happen to a healthy growing Christian who learns to confess their sins, bear fruit, give praise to God, pray according to God's will and live a contented life. When gazing at the light of a beautiful full moon, many do not realize that moon has no light of its own. The light of the moon is actually the sun's light reflecting off the moon. We are told to be the light of the world. However, we have no light other than that which is reflecting off us, which is Christ in us. Glorifying and loving God is basically the same thing. Jesus said in John 14:15 "If you love Me, you will obey what I command." It is our actions that glorify God, not our words. We glorify God by being ambassadors to this fallen world, representing Him in this sinful world. We were created by God, according to His desire, and our lives are to be lived for Him so that we might accomplish what He has for us to do.

3. You were created to praise and worship God (Psalm 86:12; 86:9). Praise means "to commend, to applaud or magnify." It is an expression of humbling ourselves and centering our attention completely upon the Lord with great love and thanksgiving. Praise is commanded by the Lord, if we don't the stones will cry out to Him (Luke 19:40). There are many actions involved with praising God—verbal expressions of adoration and thanksgiving, singing, playing instruments, shouting, dancing, lifting or clapping our hands. The purpose of our worship is to glorify, honor, praise, exalt, and please God. We are commanded to praise the Lord, "Let everything that has breath praise the Lord" (Psalm 150:6). Our worship shows our thanksgiving and loyalty to God for His grace in providing us with the way to escape the bondage of sin, so we can have salvation. The nature of the worship God demands is the humbling of our souls before Him (James 4:6, 10). Worship is a lifestyle. True worship is when you give yourself completely to God. God does not have to have our worship, but we must worship to please Him.

Our true praise and worship is designed by God to bring us closer to Him and to cause us to think more like He thinks, thus becoming more like Him. You are as close to God as you choose to be (James 4:8). Our worship not only honors and magnifies God, but it is also for our own edification and strength. Worship helps us develop God-like character. We become like those we admire and worship. When we worship God we tend to value what He values and gradually take on His characteristics and qualities. When we worship Him we develop such traits as forgiveness, tenderness, justice, righteousness, purity, kindness and love. Psalm 148:1-10 tells us that all of creation is commanded to give praise to God. Praise elevates us into God's presence and power.

Paul and Silas knew the secret of how to lift their hearts above their troubles and enter into God's presence, and power (Acts 16:22-30). Praising God should become a lifestyle (Psalm 34:1). Praise affects you. It touches everything and every part of your life. Likewise, a lack of praise affects you in a negative way. Praise will get our focus where it needs to be—on God. There will be a day when every knee will bow to praise God (Philippians 2:10-11) some joyfully giving praise others will give praise as conquered enemies headed for eternal hell.

4. You were created to grow in the fruit of the Spirit. "The fruit of the Spirit is love, joy, peace, patience, kindness, goodness, faithfulness, gentleness and self-control" (Galatians 5:22-23). These characteristics do not naturally abide in us, so they must be developed. This can only take place with the help of the Holy Spirit. The Christian life is a battle of the sinful flesh (the old nature) against the new nature (the Fruit of the Spirit) available through Christ (2 Corinthians 5:17). One of the main reasons we are here is to take on the nature of Christ, and walk in His ways. Spiritual fruit does not grow overnight, it takes time. This fruit goes against our fallen nature so it also requires the Holy Spirit's help as well as our earnest desire to conform to the image of Christ. Our highest purpose is that Christ would present the Church to the Father, holy and blameless. As part of the family of God that is our calling, to be transformed into the image of Christ. Our commitment to growth wanes easily when we become tired of waiting, but we must not become discouraged, or weary (Galatians 6:9). Rather, we must continue to do our part by laying aside our preoccupation with ourselves and focus on others—both God and our neighbors. The type of person you become is more important than your successes and failures in life. Speak the truths of God in your home, market place, workplace, and in your everyday travel on the highway and by-ways of life.

5. You were created to spread the gospel (Psalm 96:3; Isaiah 12:4; Matthew 28:19-20). This is called the "Great Commission" where Jesus commands His followers in taking the good news to the entire world. Several verses in Scripture tell us clearly that God expects us to spread His Word to everyone in the world (Mark 16:15; Matthew 24:14). We have a chance to bring others to Him by explaining biblical prophecies and to help lead them to the truth. So, as believers one of our primary goals and purposes should be to spread the gospel everywhere we go. It is God's desires that no one perish but that all come to repentance. Therefore, He has commissioned His family (that would be us) to tell the world this great truth.

6. You were created to be stewards of God's creation (Psalm 8:3-8; 115:16). The psalmist begins the 24th psalm with, "The earth is the Lord's and everything in it, the world, and all who live in it." Christian stewardship is a way of living in which we recognize that everything belongs to God. All resources must be used for His glory. A steward is someone who handles affairs for someone else. In ancient kingdoms, stewards ran the country in the absence of the king. Upon the king's return, the steward gave a full accounting for his actions.

This concept of stewardship dates from the beginning of time, when God entrusted the Earth to Adam and Eve and their offspring (Genesis 1:26-28). Collectively we have the responsibility of the Earth and also many spiritual riches to be used to advance the kingdom of God (Luke 19:11-27). While we know that a steward is one who manages the possessions of another, we are all stewards of the resources, abilities and opportunities that God has entrusted to our care.

One day each one of us will be called to give an account for how we have managed what the Master has given us. God has divided the job of stewardship among many of us so we are only responsible for a very small portion. God's goal isn't simply to keep you and your family reasonably comfortable—He has a kingdom to build, and you're a part of His management team in accomplishing that plan. The primary purpose of all creation is twofold: to give glory to God and to serve man's needs in preparation for Heaven. The created order was given by God to man so that man might achieve his temporal purpose in preparation for Heaven's glory. We need to take care of what has been entrusted to us. If all of creation gives glory to God then we are to take care of that creation for God. We are also to take care of God's creation because there will be others coming after us using the same Earth, trees, flowers, fish and animals. God says a wise hunter eats the game he kills; he doesn't just let it rot (Proverbs 12:27). The Bible tells us, "A righteous man has regard for the life of his animal (Proverbs 12:10). There are groups of people today who feel man is going to destroy the planet. I do not believe man is going to destroy the Earth, because God told us He was going to destroy the Earth and then created a new one (Revelation 21). But that does not mean we shouldn't take care of it and our environment, its air and water. This is different than the radical environmentalists who have a political agenda behind their belief and feel that man is subservient even to the animals. Many of the environmentalists are evolutionists and believe man is no more important than a chicken, just farther along in the evolutionary process. Therefore, their world-view and beliefs are based upon this premise.

7. We were created to reproduce godly offspring. "Be fruitful and multiply, and fill the Earth and subdue it" (Genesis 1:28). All of creation is designed to reproduce after its kind. Man alone was commanded not only to fill the Earth, but also to subdue it. The word subdues means: to bring into subjection; overcome, to bring under control. This requires not only bearing children, but rearing godly children who will properly subdue the Earth under God. This does not mean that every person must get married and have children to fulfill God's purpose. But it does mean that children are to be viewed as blessings from God. Our children are one of the greatest blessings and biggest responsibilities God entrusts to us. In a selfish world where many couples choose not to have children for financial reasons, we need to realize this is one of our purposes in life. Godly offspring continue the mandate to glorify God. God commanded believers to be fruitful and fill the Earth with God fearing children who will make up the Kingdom of God. The enemy of our soul has continually tried to destroy the seed of man, from Genesis on. He desires to destroy the marriage between a man and woman to eliminate the seed of man. The evil philosophy of feminism is widespread in the world and even in the church. The role of mother in the home is greatly despised in our society while the career woman is glamorized. She has made a name for herself, yet the mother who stays home to raise her children is despised or thought of as ignorant. There is a spiritual thread that runs through this new normal, and that is the destruction or elimination of the family. The family is the basic building block of the Kingdom of God and our enemy wants to weaken, destroy, or redefine it (Ephesians 5:22-33). Satan is so deceived he still thinks he can destroy or subvert God's ultimate plan for man.

8. You were created to use the talents God has given you. He tells us in Romans 12:4-8 that He has given each of us gifts and we are to develop and use them for His glory. These gifts or talents should be looked upon as investments God has given to us with expectations that His investments will multiply. Many Christians get confused because they don't know what their gifts are. There are ways to find out your gifts and fulfill your destiny!

   a. First step is to believe you were given gifts and talents from God. Then ask God for a burning desire to find them and to not settle for anything less than that.

   b. Get really good at being a Christian. Be kind to people, forgive others and learn from the Master. Our Father wants us to learn how to love and serve others and we cannot do that if we don't get along with them.

   c. As you grow in your Christian walk you will also get better at hearing from Him. Through His still small voice and the Word of God, You will hear Him. As you hear His voice better it will be much easier for Him to direct you into your purpose in life.

   d. Take the focus off yourself and begin looking for ways to be a blessing to others. Focusing on others helps you find direction for your own life. The world tells us "If you don't take care of yourself who will?" How about God? So work with God to find your life's purpose. People who manage to break out of selfishness and focus on caring for the needs of others find a sense of purpose and fulfillment far beyond any possible worldly gratification. The only way to find true happiness is to serve God, follow His ways and help those in need (Isaiah 58:10-11). Life's meaning is not found in getting more, but in giving more.

   e. Be willing to try new things that interest you—doors will either open or close.

   f. Be patient—learn to trust that God will show you when He's ready, or when He knows you are ready. God isn't going to reveal to you every piece of the puzzle all at once. If, forty years ago God had shown Bonnie and me we would be pioneering a church, we would have been stunned. He took years to develop character in us, with experience and more experience. We are not totally there yet but apparently He felt we could learn as we go for the rest of the trip.

   g. Don't waste your time on things you know aren't from God, or aren't for you. Many good things have been offered to us as a church over the years but we had to know what God has called us to do. All good things might not be God things for you.

   h. Don't let people around you talk you into things that do not fit you. Every ministry, every labor of love, every opportunity might not be the right fit for you.

   i. Don't ever give up until you find what your "sweet spot" in God's Kingdom is. The "sweet spot" is a golfing term that describes the exact spot where the club face should hit the golf ball upon contact. Unfortunately, few times do I hit that spot which means my normal shot sends the ball in many directions other than the desired or intended location. Do not give up until you find where God can use you in His Kingdom.

   j. Don't sit and wait for God to send you a text; it is easier to steer a moving vehicle than one that is parked. Find a place to start and learn as you go. While preparing this message Bonnie and I were flying back from Florida after attending our daughter's wedding. As the courtesy snack was placed on my tray the Delta airline napkin had this motto embossed on each napkin "No one changed the world by staying put." I found it appropriate to include that in this booklet.

Remember, as you search for and fulfill your gift or gifts that there are seasons of life. Your purpose may be redirected or carried out differently through different seasons of life. There was a time in my life that I worked with young boys, disciplining them in a class similar to boy scouts. Then for years I taught adult Sunday school classes, following Bible school classes, pioneering outreach ministries, missionary work, and finally pastoring.

A young mother's primary ministry is with her children, however later in life she may find a ministry within or outside the church that she has always desired to help in. A retired man or woman will find great fulfillment actively pursuing a ministry rather than sitting at home. God told us in Psalm 92:14 that "We will still bear fruit in old age" and that is very evident at Old Town.

Many people use their God given talent to pursue a secular occupation and to live the "good life" in America. God does give us gifts and talents that can be used to make a living but they were primarily given to fulfill your life's destiny and to create a legacy. Bonnie and I have led teams of professionals (doctors, dentists, carpenters, nurses, masons, electricians, and teachers) to several different countries where they volunteered their time and skills to help others and to651 build the Kingdom of God.

Many famous and successful people have reached the top of their field and declared the success to be meaningless. There is a much deeper need that success just doesn't fill. Purpose is perhaps one of the deepest human longings. Only in Christ can we fulfill our purpose in life. Only in Christ can we leave a lasting legacy.

Most people want to be successful in life. But what is success? Webster tells us success is: The gaining of position, fame, prosperity, wealth, achievement, and station in life. This is the so called "American Dream." Webster's definition is man's definition about purpose in life. Suppose we re-define success using God's purpose for life. What would that look like? Success in God's eyes is much different than that of our fallen world. A simple formula for determining God's success is the ratio of talents used to talents received. King David told his son Solomon, do what the Lord commands you and you will be a success (I Kings 2:3). Once becoming a Christian and in the process of learning to follow and obeying Christ the measure of success will be how you use the gifts and talents given to you.

God has a plan and purpose for each person's life, whether or not we fulfill that purpose is up to us.

a. He had a plan for Adam (Genesis 1:28).
b. He had a plan for Abraham (Genesis 12:1-3).
c. He had a plan for Joseph (Genesis 45:4-9).
d. He had a plan for Israel (Genesis 50:24; Exodus 6:6-8).
e. He had a plan for Jesus (Luke 18:31-33).
f. He had a plan for Paul (Acts 22:14-15, 26:16-19).
g. He has a plan for each one of us (Ephesians 2:10, 3:11, Jeremiah 29:11).

There are some who feel we have little or no part in that plan, because it was preordained of God and will take place regardless of what we do. I do not see that in scripture, the Bible clearly teaches we have a part in that plan. Yes, God has a plan for every one of our lives but we can reject His plan and live our plan if it is what we desire. Even Jesus had to choose whether or not to fulfill His Fathers purpose and plan. In the Garden of Gethsemane He had to do His Fathers will and not His own. He could not stand the thought of being separated from His Father but said, "My Father, if it is possible, let this cup pass from Me; yet not as I will, but as You will," (Matthew 26:39). We also need to find and fulfill our God given purpose in life and must say to God, "Let Your will be done in my life not my will." Then at the end of this earthly life we will have no regrets and with honor and excitement enter into our eternal state with our Father.

Kingdom Quiz (What is the Purpose of Life?)

1. Does God really have a purpose for our life?

2. Does He have a purpose for you?

3. Is your purpose in life simply to be happy?

4. Where do we look to find our purpose?

5. What is the difference between your general purpose and your specific purpose?

6. Has God given you specific gifts and talents to find and use for His Kingdom? (Jeremiah 29:11)

7. This life is preparation for _____.

Proof of God

Is there actual proof that God exists, and that Jesus actually lived on this earth?

Many people do not believe there is a God; they are called atheists. Others call themselves agnostics, which means they believe that nothing is known of the existence of God. This person claims neither faith nor disbelief in God. While I will show an overwhelming amount of evidence to prove there is a God, I also realize many people will continue to believe what they want even in the face of the overwhelming evidence. This fact is the wonder of God who even allows us to deny Him if we so choose. However, there are grave consequences for this decision. To help clear this up let's research the subject of our Savior and God. Is there proof or evidence that Jesus really lived, died and rose again? Is there proof that God exists?

As Christians, we need to realize that not everyone believes the Bible as we do. Most Christians do not realize all the available evidence that proves Jesus lived on this earth, then died, and rose again. These facts can be proven without even using the Bible. These facts about Jesus are the central truth of the entire Bible. When these facts are proven, who could walk away from God?

Jesus died to pay for our sins, rose again and became the first of millions who will come back to life again.

As a retired police detective sergeant, I want to collect and explain some of these proofs. I understand though, for some people, all the evidence in the world will not change their opinions and beliefs. What are these proofs?

1. We have written historical evidence that Jesus lived 2,000 years ago. This evidence is not simply from the Bible but from historians and other authors, many of whom were not even believers. These writings can withstand the test of credibility and the ancient writing rule.
2. There is eyewitness testimony from those present at Jesus' death. These witnesses would pass the test of credibility as they had no reason to lie. Many of them suffered death for their testimony.
3. There was an empty tomb. No one has ever discovered the body of Jesus after His death, not even to this day.
4. There is geographic evidence. All the cities and locations listed in the Bible are real places, just as indicated in the Bible and they have been discovered after thousands of years.
5. There is archaeological evidence. There are numerous archaeological discoveries which show the reality of the Gospel narratives. Sir William Ramsay, regarded as one of the greatest archaeologists ever, was trained in mid-nineteenth century German historical skepticism. He did not believe that the New Testament documents were historically reliable. However, his archaeological investigations drove him to see that his skepticism was unwarranted. He had a profound change of attitude. Speaking of Luke, the writer of the Gospel of Luke and the Acts of the Apostles, Ramsay said, 'Luke is a historian of the first rank…he should be placed along with the greatest of historians.'
6. All the Biblical prophecies in the Old Testament telling of the coming Messiah were fulfilled in Jesus.
7. The Bibles is historically accurate. Nelson Glueck, famous Jewish archaeologist, spoke of what he called 'the most incredibly accurate historical memory of the Bible, and particularly so when it is fortified by archaeologist fact'. Discovery after discovery has established the accuracy of innumerable details, and has brought increased recognition to the value of the Bible as a source of history. There is more than enough evidence to prove Jesus lived, died, and was alive after He died. A jury deciding this evidence would just need to consist of 12 reasonable people. They don't even need to be Christians. This evidence proves the core of the Gospel; the reason Jesus came and died.

While we know that Jesus was God in the flesh, we can also prove the invisible God who is present with us continually.

The proof that God exists is incredible.

8. Albert Einstein said, "The harmony of natural law reveals an intelligence of such superiority that compared with it all the systematic thinking of human beings is utterly insignificant."

9. Isaac Newton's Third Law of Motion states that, "with every action there is an opposite and equal reaction." He tells us "force comes in pairs." From any effect whatsoever it can be proven that a corresponding cause exists. If only the effects of it are sufficiently known to us, for since effects depend on causes, the effect being given, it is necessary that a preceding cause exists. So we know God exists, although He is not seen by our eyes. He is provable through effects that are known to us.

Using Newton's Law of Motion, everything which comes into existence is caused to exist by something else.

What caused the universe? Did it just pop into existence? Just as 0=0, nothing can come from nothing. For something to come into existence, there must be something else that already exists that can bring it into existence. Remember, that for every action there is always a reaction. The fact that the universe began to exist implies that something brought it into existence, that the universe has a Creator. Every cause must be at least as great as the effect it produces and will, in reality, produce an effect that is less than itself.

The Apostle Paul (Romans 1:20) tells us, "The unseen things of God are visible through His manifest works." His magnificent works prove He exists. So from the works of God His existence can be proved.

10. Another proof that God exists is what we observe in the universe (Psalms 19:1). The heavens declare the existence of God.

11. Another source of proof is that God has taken the initiative to step into the universe to reveal Himself. That first Christmas was proof of His love for every person on earth.

12. Another proof of the existence of God is the order in the universe. The Anthropic Principle is the Law of human existence. This principle or law states the existence of this universe is impossible and cannot happen by chance. That God fine-tuned the universe for our existence. This is seen in the complexity and intricacy of the universe. The complexity of our planet points to a deliberate Designer who, not only created our universe, but sustains it today. For instance, the earth is the perfect size. It's size and corresponding gravity holds a thin layer of mostly nitrogen and oxygen gases, only extending about 50 miles above the earth's surface. If earth were smaller, the atmosphere would be impossible to sustain life, like the planet Mercury. If earth were larger, its atmosphere would be like Jupiter.

The earth has a precise 23.5 degree tilt from true vertical. Scientists have determined that as little as one half a degree change in either direction would result in our freezing to death or burning up.

If the moon were one degree farther from or closer to earth, our coastal cities would be underwater every twelve hours.

Thanks to the orbiting Hubble Space Telescope, astronomers have discovered that each star possesses its own color spectrum and no two of them are alike.

Listen to the uniqueness of our Creator who designed us specifically for Himself:

No two leaves are alike.

No two blades of grass are alike.

No two snowflakes are alike.

Watermelons always have either ten or twelve stripes.

Each ear of corn always has an even number of rows.

No human has the same fingerprint or DNA.

But the pinnacle of God's Creation: of all the billions of people who have lived before us on this earth, of all the billions that are here now, and of all the billions that will come after us, there has never been, there is not one now, nor will there ever be another human being like you. How can we ignore a Creator like our God? The extreme improbability that so many variables would align so perfectly in our favor merely by chance has led some scientists and philosophers to propose instead that it was God who providentially engineered the universe to suit our specific needs. That is the Anthropic Principle.

13. Another proof of God is when an individual experiences events that could only be caused by God, i.e. miracles.

The universe had a start; only God could do that. There is no Big Bang theory, God spoke it into existence.

14. The DNA code is proof of God's existence. Someone who writes an instruction manual does so with purpose. Every cell of our bodies contains a very detailed instruction code, which is more complicated than our minds or our computers can comprehend. The human body is comprised of millions of irreducibly complex parts that could never have evolved over time.

15. Another one of the greatest proofs of God are the lives that have been changed through serving and living for Him. My life and countless others have changed directions once coming to understand the reality of God.

16. The Second Law of Thermodynamics proves the existence of God. This law states that systems spontaneously evolve towards states of higher entropy. Entropy means the degree of disorder in a system. In other words, the amount of disorder always increases with time. Things progress naturally from order to disorder or from an available energy state to one where energy is less available. A good example: a hot cup of coffee cools off in an insulated room. The total amount of energy in the room remains the same. Energy is not lost; it is simply transferred (in the form of heat) from the hot coffee to the cool air, warming up the air slightly. When the coffee is hot, there is available energy because of the temperature difference between the coffee and the air. When the coffee is room temperature, there is no temperature difference between the coffee and the air, i.e. the energy is all in an unavailable state. The system is "dead" because no further work can be done since there is no more available energy. The second law says that the reverse cannot happen. Now consider the entire universe as one giant system. Stars are hot, just like the cup of coffee, and are cooling down, losing energy into space. The hot stars in cooler space represent a state of available energy, just like the hot coffee in the room. However, the

second law of thermodynamics requires that this available energy is constantly changing to unavailable energy. In another analogy, the entire universe is winding down like a giant wind-up clock, ticking down and losing available energy. Since energy is continually changing from available to unavailable energy, someone had to give it available energy in the beginning. Someone had to wind up the clock of the universe at the beginning. Only the creator of the second law of thermodynamics could violate the second law of thermodynamics, and create energy in a state of availability in the first place. Which also means, the present universe, as we know it, cannot last forever. It also means that it did not evolve from a simpler form of life to a more complex for of life (i.e. evolution) which would violate this second law of thermodynamics.

With all the proof we have, it still takes a step of faith to accept the Savior of the world into your life.

We know God exists because He pursues us.

Kingdom Quiz (Proof of God)

1. Can the life and death and resurrection of Jesus be proven today in court?
2. Is there other written material besides the Bible that tells us about Jesus?
4. What is Isaac Newton's Third Law of Motion?
5. How does Newton's Third Law of Motion apply to proving God exists?
6. What is the Anthropic Principle?
7. How is the DNA code proof of God's existence?

Closing

As a Christian, how should I respond to my teacher when he/she teaches on evolution?

First and foremost you should not be disrespectful. You will need to listen to and take tests on the subjects they teach even though you may not agree with the teaching.

When you have an opportunity to speak, or can create an opportunity to speak, explain how you disagree with the theory or write it on the back of your paper.

Your teacher may say, "Is it because you are a Christian?"

I would say something like this, "No it isn't because I am a Christian, although I am one, it is because it doesn't make sense and lacks evidence to prove its theory.

As Christians we are not afraid of others opposing views. The Bible tells us most people are not Christians and do not hold to our view of life (Matthew 7:13-14). Christianity can stand up against any and all other views of the origin and purpose of life. But what we are opposed to is a theory taught as proof positive and that does not allow Creation a place at the table. As a Christian, I'm not afraid to put my belief up against an ardent evolutionist, but an evolutionist is afraid to put their belief up against a Creationist. That is why schools and universities refuse to allow Creationists a place at the table of ideas and beliefs.